MOVIE ★ ICONS

SINATRA

EDITOR
PAUL DUNCAN

TEXT
ALAIN SILVER

PHOTOS
THE KOBAL COLLECTION

TASCHEN

HONG KONG KÖLN LONDON LOS ANGELES MADRID PARIS TOKYO

CONTENTS

1

FRANK SINATRA: THE VOICE

BY ALAIN SILVER

FRANK SINATRA: DIE STIMME

FRANK SINATRA: LA VOIX

FRANK SINATRA: THE VOICE

by Alain Silver

Frank Sinatra's voice has arguably been heard more often than that of any other person in the history of sound recording. As an icon in the 1990s, Sinatra was at once *éminence grise*, the godfather of pop, and a performer with the same assurance as the rail-thin young man who had won an amateur singing context six decades earlier. Long before he was chairman of the board, Frank Sinatra was a child of the jazz age and its freewheeling approach to life. In the course of a meteoric rise from singing waiter to the world's first pop star, whose appeal ranged from bobbysoxers to society matrons as he made 'Swoonatra' a phenomenon, Sinatra relied on his own version of keeping it simple: "I'm not one of those complicated, mixed-up cats. I'm not looking for the secret to life or the answer to life. I just go on from day to day taking what comes."

As an entertainer Sinatra was both a visionary and a pragmatist, a prototype for the 20th-century man. While many stars in one creative discipline have had crossover success in another, only a handful have ever attempted (let alone equaled) the accomplishments of Frank Sinatra as a singer, actor, producer of albums and motion pictures, philanthropist, lothario, and even film director. "Let's face it," said Bing Crosby, the crooner who inspired the young Frank, "Sinatra is the king. He's a very sharp operator, and has a keen appreciation of what the public wants." In fact, as a man who professed that "you have to scrape bottom to appreciate life and start living again," Sinatra understood that determination was the bedrock of any achievement. So it might be more accurate to say that it was, first, always about what Sinatra and not the public wanted and, second, it was about him selling band leaders, studio chiefs, impresarios, and ultimately the audience on the fact that they wanted it too. While Sinatra did not always succeed at whatever he decided to try, his failures were few.

In 1952, when facing damage to his vocal cords that could possibly end his singing career, Sinatra fought against long odds to win the part of Maggio in *From Here to Eternity*. "His fervor,

PORTRAIT (1951)

"You've got to love living, because dying is a pain in the ass."
Frank Sinatra

his anger, his bitterness had something to do with the character of Maggio, but also with what he had gone through the last number of years," remarked his co-star Burt Lancaster, "You knew this was a raging little man who was at the same time a good human being." As with any artist who becomes an icon, Sinatra took one of life's unforeseen vicissitudes and transformed it into an even more unexpected triumph: an Academy Award for a dramatic performance.

From that point Sinatra would never be pigeonholed again as a crooner capable only of light comedy. Certainly he continued to make comedies and musicals as he branched out into action films and Westerns and more somber dramas. Two years after the accolades for *From Here to Eternity* when he co-starred with Marlon Brando in *Guys and Dolls*, Sinatra emphatically demonstrated how rare it was for actors who had won Academy Awards to be able to sing. For Sinatra no reinvention of himself was ever a question of changing styles, of changing who he was as a human being, but of adding a new spin and keeping it honest, because as he often professed, "You can be the most artistically perfect performer in the world, but an audience is like a broad. If you're indifferent: Endsville."

For Sinatra not being a complicated or mixed-up cat meant just that, and the key to success was to express himself with unflinching honesty. He took this seriousness into every aspect of his life. When he stepped into the complex and uncertain world of motion pictures first as actor, then producer, and eventually director of a groundbreaking film, Sinatra never forgot that "luck is only important in so far as getting the chance to sell yourself at the right moment. After that, you've got to have talent and know how to use it."

All who knew Sinatra and those who knew him best realized that what he had was more than just talent, that his casual demeanor and ease at living belied his passion and his artistry, that he took what came and made it work, always understanding the irony that "You only live once, and the way I live, once is enough."

FRANK SINATRA: DIE STIMME

von Alain Silver

Man kann wohl behaupten, dass man Frank Sinatras Stimme häufiger gehört hat als irgendeine andere in der Geschichte der Tonaufnahme. Als Ikone war Sinatra in den neunziger Jahren des letzten Jahrhunderts zugleich Künstler, graue Eminenz und Pate des Pop mit der gleichen Selbstsicherheit wie jener spindeldürre junge Mann, der sechs Jahrzehnte zuvor einen Gesangswettbewerb für Amateure gewonnen hatte. Lange bevor er der „Vorstandsvorsitzende des Showbusiness" wurde, war Frank Sinatra ein Kind des Jazz-Zeitalters und dessen ungezwungener Lebenseinstellung. Im Verlauf eines kometenhaften Aufstiegs vom singenden Kellner zum ersten Popstar der Welt, der Backfische genauso mitriss wie Damen der feinen Gesellschaft und „Swoonatra" (to swoon = „in Ohnmacht fallen") zum gesellschaftlichen Phänomen machte, verließ sich Sinatra ganz auf seine eigene Philosophie: „Ich gehöre nicht zu diesen komplizierten, wirren Typen. Ich versuche nicht, das Geheimnis des Lebens oder den Sinn des Daseins zu ergründen. Ich lebe einfach in den Tag hinein und nehme, was da kommt."

Als Entertainer war Sinatra sowohl Visionär als auch Pragmatiker, also ein Prototyp für den Menschen des 20. Jahrhunderts. Wenngleich viele Stars einer schöpferischen Disziplin auch noch in einer zweiten erfolgreich waren, konnte nur eine Handvoll mit Frank Sinatras Leistungen als Sänger, Schauspieler, Schallplatten- und Filmproduzent, Philanthrop, Schürzenjäger und sogar Filmregisseur Schritt halten, und die wenigsten hatten dabei einen solchen Erfolg. „Geben wir's zu", meinte Bing Crosby, der den jungen Frank einst gesanglich inspiriert hatte, „Sinatra ist der König. Er ist ein sehr cleverer Macher und hat ein sehr feines Gespür dafür, was das Publikum will". Als ein Mann, der gestand, dass man „ganz am Boden sein [muss], um das Leben schätzen zu lernen und wieder neu aufzuleben", wusste Sinatra tatsächlich sehr gut, dass Entschlossenheit das Fundament eines jeden Erfolgs war. Es wäre vielleicht zutreffender zu sagen, dass es immer in erster Linie um das ging, was Sinatra selbst wollte, nicht um das Publikum, und dass er den Bandleadern, Studiobossen, Konzertagenten und schließ-

STILL FROM 'VON RYAN'S EXPRESS' (1965)

„Man muss das Leben schon lieben, denn sterben ist ganz schön scheiße."
Frank Sinatra

lich auch dem Publikum einredete, dass sie das gleiche wollten. Auch wenn Sinatra nicht mit allem, was er anfasste, Erfolg hatte, so waren seine Misserfolge doch kaum der Rede wert.

Als er sich 1952 eine Stimmbandverletzung zuzog, die seine Gesangskarriere hätte beenden können, kämpfte er gegen viele Widerstände, um die Rolle des Gefreiten Maggio in *Verdammt in alle Ewigkeit* spielen zu dürfen. „Seine Leidenschaft, sein Zorn, seine Bitterkeit hatten etwas mit der Figur des Maggio gemeinsam, aber auch das, was er in den letzten Jahren durchgemacht hatte", erklärte sein Kollege Burt Lancaster. „Man wusste, dass dies ein wütender kleiner Mann, aber zugleich ein guter Mensch war." Wie jeder Künstler, der zur Ikone wird, packte Sinatra eine unerwartete Gelegenheit beim Schopf und verwandelte sie in einen noch weniger vorhersehbaren Triumph: einen „Oscar" für eine Dramarolle.

Von diesem Zeitpunkt an steckte man Sinatra nie wieder in die Schublade des Sängers, der allenfalls zu ein paar anspruchslosen Lustspielrollen fähig war. Freilich drehte er weiterhin Komödien und Musicals, aber nebenbei versuchte er sich auch in Actionfilmen, Western und düsteren Dramen. Zwei Jahre nach dem Ritterschlag für *Verdammt in alle Ewigkeit*, als er neben Marlon Brando in *Schwere Jungen, leichte Mädchen* spielte, machte Sinatra überdeutlich, wie selten es war, dass Schauspieler, die mit einem Academy Award ausgezeichnet worden waren, auch singen konnten. Sinatra erfand sich immer wieder neu, aber dazu musste er seinen Stil oder sich selbst als Mensch nicht ändern, sondern er gab all dem nur eine neue Wendung und blieb sich treu, denn er sagte oft: „Künstlerisch kann man der perfekteste Darsteller der Welt sein, aber das Publikum ist wie eine Frau. Wenn man gleichgültig ist: Feierabend!"

Für Sinatra bedeutete dies, nicht kompliziert oder verworren zu sein – und der Schlüssel zu seinem Erfolg war, dass er sich mit unverstellter Ehrlichkeit ausdrückte. Er übertrug seine Ernsthaftigkeit auf sämtliche Bereiche seines Lebens. Während er in die komplexe und unsichere Welt des Films vorstieß – erst als Schauspieler, dann als Produzent und schließlich als Regisseur eines bahnbrechenden Films –, vergaß Sinatra niemals, dass „Glück nur insofern eine Rolle spielt, als dass es einem die Chance gibt, sich im richtigen Augenblick zu verkaufen. Danach muss man Talent besitzen und wissen, wie man es einsetzt".

Alle, die Sinatra kannten und vor allem die, die ihn am besten kannten, wussten, dass er mehr besaß als nur Talent, dass seine lockere Art und Lebensweise leicht über seine Leidenschaft und seine künstlerischen Fähigkeiten hinwegtäuschten, dass er nahm, was kam, und dass er etwas daraus machte, weil er stets die Ironie des Lebens verstand: „Man lebt nur einmal, und so wie ich lebe, ist einmal auch genug."

ON THE SET OF 'ON THE TOWN' (1949)

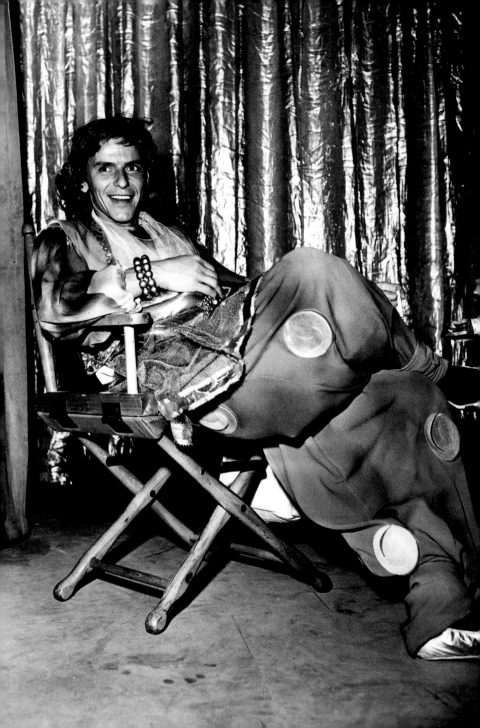

FRANK SINATRA : LA VOIX

Alain Silver

La voix de Frank Sinatra est sans doute celle qu'on a le plus entendue depuis l'invention du microsillon. En 1990, l'homme fait figure d'icône : il est à la fois l'éminence grise et le parrain de la musique pop tout en restant l'artiste de variétés sûr de lui, aussi confiant que le jeune homme filiforme qui a triomphé à un concours de chant amateur soixante ans plus tôt. La cigale s'est muée en fourmi, Sinatra est désormais surnommé « The Chairman of the Board », mais il n'en demeure pas moins l'héritier insouciant des années jazz. Ce garçon de restaurant passionné de chant est devenu la plus grande vedette de la pop, capable de séduire aussi bien les midinettes que les dames patronnesses. Pourtant, tout au long de sa fulgurante ascension, « Swoonatra » (de l'anglais swoon, s'évanouir) s'est efforcé de voir les choses avec simplicité. « Je n'appartiens pas à la race des esprits compliqués et sans repères. Je n'attends pas de l'existence qu'elle me livre son secret, ni même qu'elle m'apporte des réponses. Je vis au jour le jour et je me contente de profiter de ce qui se présente. »

Frank Sinatra incarne l'artiste du XXᵉ siècle, à la fois visionnaire et pragmatique. Nombre de ses pairs ont réussi dans une discipline mais n'ont obtenu qu'un demi succès dans une autre et parmi les rares qui se sont essayés à plusieurs, seule une poignée est parvenue à égaler les prouesses du Sinatra chanteur, producteur de disques et de films, philanthrope, séducteur et même réalisateur. Le crooner Bing Crosby, qui fut son modèle, disait de lui : « Tout bien considéré, Sinatra est un maître. C'est un fin stratège, et il sait exactement ce qu'attend le public. » En vérité, quand Sinatra affirme « qu'il faut toucher le fond pour apprécier la vie à sa juste valeur et renaître », il donne à entendre que la détermination est la condition de toute réussite. Au-delà des attentes du public, ce qui l'emporte, c'est ce que lui-même a choisi. Il lui reste alors à convaincre les musiciens, les directeurs de studios, les impresarios et même les auditeurs qu'eux aussi veulent la même chose. Ses tentatives n'ont pas toutes été couronnées de succès mais ses échecs se comptent sur les doigts de la main.

FRANK SINATRA & AVA GARDNER (1950)

« Il y a intérêt à aimer la vie, parce que la mort, c'est nul à ch … ! »
Frank Sinatra

En 1952, il voit sa carrière de chanteur menacée par un grave problème de cordes vocales. Sinatra entreprend alors une lutte acharnée pour obtenir le rôle de Maggio dans le film *Tant qu'il y aura des hommes*. Burt Lancaster, son partenaire à l'écran, notera plus tard que son enthousiasme, sa colère, son amertume, trouvaient un écho dans le personnage de Maggio et reflétaient les épreuves qu'il venait de traverser : « Ce petit bonhomme avait la rage au ventre, mais c'était un type généreux et ça se sentait. » Comme tous les artistes qui deviendront des icônes, Sinatra sait profiter d'une difficulté inattendue pour se tailler un succès imprévisible : l'oscar du Meilleur second rôle dans un film dramatique.

Partant de là, Frank Sinatra se débarrasse de l'image contraignante du crooner condamné à ne jouer que les héros de comédies. Sans renoncer au genre léger, il continue à tourner dans des comédies musicales tout en se lançant dans des films d'action, des westerns et des drames encore plus sombres. Deux ans après l'oscar reçu pour *Tant qu'il y aura des hommes*, il joue aux côtés de Marlon Brando dans *Blanches colombes et vilains messieurs* et prouve sans conteste combien il est rare qu'un acteur titulaire de la plus haute récompense sache également chanter. Pour lui, se réinventer ne signifie pas changer de style, ni se renier, mais expérimenter d'autres formes artistiques sans jamais tricher. Il avait coutume de dire : « Le public réagit comme les femmes. L'artiste, aussi brillant et accompli soit-il, s'il n'est pas sincère, c'en est fini de lui. »

Sinatra l'avait bien compris, il ne faut pas chercher à compliquer les choses ni trop s'écouter. La clé de son succès fut de s'exprimer avec une honnêteté indéfectible et de rester sincère en toutes circonstances. Entré dans l'univers incertain du cinéma, d'abord acteur, puis producteur et même réalisateur d'un film révolutionnaire, il n'oubliera jamais que « la chance intervient dans la mesure où elle vous permet d'être là au bon moment. Ensuite il faut avoir du talent et savoir s'en servir à bon escient ».

Tous les proches de Sinatra et surtout ses intimes ont compris qu'il avait plus que du talent et que sous son apparente simplicité, son côté bon enfant, se cachait une nature passionnée, un très grand mérite et la faculté de faire feu de tout bois. Ceux-là et ceux-là seuls ont saisi toute l'ironie de sa formule : « On ne vit qu'une fois, mais quand on vit à mon rythme, une fois suffit. »

PAGE 22
PORTRAIT
Color portrait of a very young "ol' blue eyes." /
Farbporträt eines sehr jungen „Ol' Blue Eyes". /
Portrait en couleur du beau jeune homme aux yeux
bleus que l'on surnomme « ol' blue eyes ».

PORTRAIT

2

VISUAL FILMOGRAPHY

FILMOGRAFIE IN BILDERN

FILMOGRAPHIE EN IMAGES

STILL FROM 'LAS VEGAS NIGHTS' (1941)
Before Hollywood called, Sinatra's time with the Dorsey
orchestra made him a singing star. Four years later he
would be the highest-paid entertainer in the world. /
Bevor er dem Ruf Hollywoods folgte, wurde Sinatra
bereits als Sänger im Dorsey-Orchester zum Star. Vier
Jahre später war er der höchstbezahlte Unterhaltungs-
künstler der Welt. / Avant d'être sollicité par Hollywood,
Sinatra mène déjà une brillante carrière de chanteur
avec l'orchestre de T. Dorsey. Quatre ans plus tard, il est
l'artiste de variétés le mieux payé au monde.

"The thing that influenced me most was the way
Tommy [Dorsey] played his trombone. It was my
idea to make my voice work in the same way as
a trombone or violin — not sounding like them, but
'playing' the voice like those instruments."
Frank Sinatra

„Was mich am meisten beeinflusst hat, war, wie
Tommy [Dorsey] seine Posaune spielte. Es war
meine Idee, meine Stimme genau so wirken zu
lassen wie eine Posaune oder eine Geige – nicht,
sich so anzuhören, aber die Stimme wie diese
Instrumente zu ‚spielen'."
Frank Sinatra

STILL FROM 'HIGHER AND HIGHER' (1943)
Many early movie 'roles' were as himself and often in his
musician's 'uniform.' Here Frank accompanies French
actress Michèle Morgan. / In vielen seiner frühen Film-
„Rollen" spielte er sich selbst und trug dabei meist die
„Uniform" der Musiker. Hier begleitet Frank die
französische Schauspielerin Michèle Morgan. / Dans la
plupart de ses premiers films, Sinatra incarne son
propre personnage, le plus souvent vêtu de son
« costume » de musicien. Ici, Frank a pour partenaire
l'actrice française Michèle Morgan.

« J'ai été très marqué par le jeu de Tommy
[Dorsey]. C'est en l'écoutant que m'est venue l'idée
de me servir de ma voix comme d'un trombone ou
d'un violon, pas pour en tirer les mêmes sonorités
mais pour en "jouer" comme on joue d'un de ces
instruments. »
Frank Sinatra

STILL FROM 'STEP LIVELY' (1944)
Sinatra is a playwright (hence the typewriter) visiting a cash-poor impresario who has turned Sinatra's serious play into a musical comedy. / In der Rolle eines Schriftstellers besucht Sinatra einen abgebrannten Impresario, der sein ernsthaftes Drama in ein musikalisches Lustspiel umgewandelt hat. / Sinatra incarne un auteur dramatique qui découvre qu'un impresario (fauché) a adapté sa pièce — œuvre sérieuse — pour en faire une comédie musicale.

PAGES 28/29
STILL FROM 'STEP LIVELY' (1944)
The playwright saves the day because he can sing like Sinatra. This is the 'Black and White' number. / Der Dramatiker rettet die ganze Sache, weil er singen kann wie Frank Sinatra! / L'auteur de théâtre sauve la mise parce que, comme Sinatra, il sait chanter.

STILL FROM 'STEP LIVELY' (1944)
Even in character, Sinatra was often pictured with lovely young women, like vivacious ingenue Anne Jeffries. / Selbst in seinen Rollen zeigte man Sinatra in Gesellschaft reizender junger Damen wie der lebhaften, aber naiven Miss Abbott (Anne Jeffries). / Au cinéma comme dans la vie, Sinatra apparaît souvent aux côtés de ravissantes créatures telles que la jeune et sémillante Anne Jeffries.

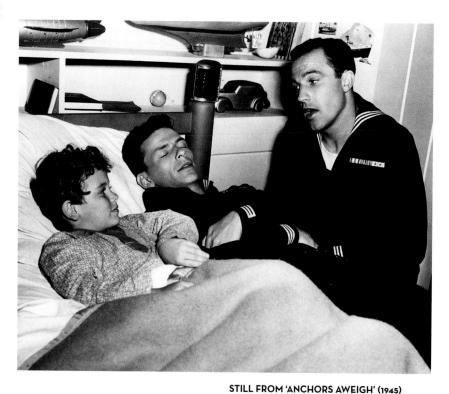

STILL FROM 'ANCHORS AWEIGH' (1945)
Even asleep between Dean Stockwell and Kelly, Sinatra
was comfortable in the center of the picture. / Selbst
schlafend zwischen Dean Stockwell und Gene Kelly
fühlte sich Sinatra im Mittelpunkt des Films sehr wohl. /
Même endormi entre Dean Stockwell et Kelly, Sinatra
fait bonne figure au centre de l'image.

STILL FROM 'ANCHORS AWEIGH' (1945)
A meatier part for MGM opposite Gene Kelly
permitted Sinatra to display singing and acting abilities.
Kelly taught Sinatra how to dance. / In diesem Film für
MGM darf Sinatra neben Gene Kelly etwas mehr von
seinem Gesangs- und Schauspieltalent zeigen. Kelly
brachte Sinatra das Tanzen bei. / Un rôle plus consistant
à la Metro Goldwyn Mayer lui offre l'occasion de
montrer ses talents de chanteur et d'acteur. Son
partenaire, Gene Kelly, lui apprend à danser.

PAGES 32/33
STILL FROM 'ANCHORS AWEIGH' (1945)
The object of the sailors' desire is Ava Gardner –
Sinatra and Gardner would later meet and marry in real
life. / Sämtliche Matrosen lüsteten nach Ava Gardner,
die Sinatra im richtigen Leben später tatsächlich
kennenlernte und sogar heiratete. / Les marins n'ont
d'yeux que pour Ava Gardner. Sinatra l'épousera
quelques années plus tard.

ON THE SET OF 'THE HOUSE I LIVE IN' (1945)
Sinatra fought for racial equality throughout his life,
which is why he originated and appeared in this
Academy Award-winning short film for director Mervyn
LeRoy (left). / Sinatra setzte sich sein ganzes Leben
lang für die Gleichbehandlung der Rassen ein, weshalb
er auch diesen mit einem Academy Award ausgezeichneten Kurzfilm unter der Regie von Mervyn LeRoy
(links) anregte und darin auftrat. / Toute sa vie durant,
Sinatra s'est battu pour l'égalité des races, d'où l'idée de
ce court métrage dans lequel il joue et qui valut un
oscar à son réalisateur, Mervyn LeRoy, (à gauche).

*"Even then you could see this boy was tough.
If you crossed him you were dead. And he couldn't
stand phonies. But if you were friends, that was it."*
Lee Castle, trumpeter for Tommy Dorsey

*„Damals konnte man schon sehen, dass das ein
harter Bursche war. Wenn man ihm in die Quere
kam, war man ein toter Mann. Und er hasste
falsche Fuffziger. Aber wenn man sein Freund war,
dann war's das."*
Lee Castle, Trompeter für Tommy Dorsey

STILL FROM 'TILL THE CLOUDS ROLL BY' (1946)
This musical pastiche featured a multitude of singers performing Jerome Kern songs. Sinatra sings 'Ol' Man River.' / In dieser musikalischen Collage traten zahlreiche Sänger auf und sangen Lieder von Jerome Kern. Sinatra singt hier „Ol' Man River". / Dans ce pastiche musical, divers artistes interprètent des chansons de Jerome Kern. Sinatra, lui, chante « Ol' Man River ».

PAGES 36/37
PAGES FROM 'PHOTOPLAY' (1945)

« *Déjà à l'époque on sentait que ce type était un dur, un vrai. Il ne supportait pas les faux jetons. Si tu le contrariais, t'étais un homme mort. Mais si t'étais son pote, c'était pour la vie.* »
Lee Castle, trompettiste dans l'orchestre de Tommy Dorsey

BEGINNING

A vital and significant series
by Frank Sinatra
for young Americans

I WANT TO TALK TO

"You'll find you're much surer of getting whatever you want—if you'll go
after it in a decent way," says Frank, shown here talking to youthful editors

HIYA, Kids. . . .
Guess I'm a little out of my
element in this writing business
but I figured here in Photoplay I
could talk to two or three million
of you at once. In the series of talks
I gave at schools a month or two ago
I only got to talk to a few thousand
of you at best. And I didn't begin
to cover the questions you've been
asking in your letters lately. Stands
to reason I can't answer all of you
personally. I'd be an old graybeard
before I got through. Besides, most
of the time you tell me not to write
to you anyway—that getting your
problem on paper has helped—and if
anyone in your family got my letter
you'd get the devil or the horse-
laugh.

So many of you write explaining
you're not JDs. I know that, Kids.
It doesn't make you a juvenile delin-
quent to go around in bobby socks
and sloppy joes, to talk and dance
jive, to make an idol of somebody in
a band or athletics or public life, to
collect autographs, to keep scrap
books. It doesn't even make you a
JD to stay out late once in a while,
or skip school now and then or get
chased by the neighborhood cop oc-
casionally. It is stupid, however, to
do these things. Because there's always the danger they'll become a
habit—habits which may very well
turn you into a JD in time—habits
which will be anything but assets
when you are older.

But I don't have to go on. You
know what you do. So you know if
you're a JD. Or just a healthy nor-
mal American kid. And don't get to
thinking, "So I'm a juvenile delin-
quent, am I? Okay! I'll give them
what they expect. I'll have all the
fun and let someone else do the
worrying!"

Because, I'm telling you, it won't
work out that way. It'll work out
with you doing worse and worse
things and having less and less fun—
and ending up caring and worrying
plenty. Plenty!

Nobody needs to tell you when
you're doing wrong. As I found out
a long time ago, we all have some-

thing inside of us that tries to steer
us right. Sometimes we ignore that
voice or whatever it is and go ahead
anyhow. But this never means we
can't still right-about-face. This
never means we can't say to our-
selves and anyone else whose business it is, "That's not for me! No
more!"

I don't mean to go off on any spree
of "Dos and Don'ts." I did a lot of
things as a kid that were wrong, even
had fun doing some of them. And
plenty of times when my father gave
me a bawling out I went off sulking
and said to myself, "There's a lot I
could tell my old man—with his old-
fashioned ideas." I don't suppose
there's ever been a kid who didn't
think he knew more than his mother
and father.

I had a terrific knack for getting
into trouble; probably because I
hung out with older fellows and, a
little tyke anyhow, was always the
last guy to get away. . . .

Like the time a bunch of us decided to raid a fruit stand. We
waited until it got pretty dark, then
struck out across the street. While
the old fruit man had his back turned
we charged his stand with loud
whoops. Then we jumped in and
grabbed. Anything we could lay our
hands on. Mostly things we couldn't
do anything with, it turned out, like
spinach or cabbage or potatoes.

When a cop came down the street
the other fellows beat it. I knew I
didn't have a chance of keeping up

Frankie, aged six, and his cousin
at the Sinatra home in Hoboken

with them so I ducked under th
stand. And there I had to stay f
about three hours; until twel
o'clock when the cop finally ga
up waiting around in case the oth
fellows came back and the old fru
man closed up and went home.

The moral of all this is that I ha

You!

Frankie, who played hooky, got chased by cops and ran away from home, knows whereof he speaks

BY FRANK SINATRA

Frankie, rear right, and some of his gang, on a New Jersey beach

nothing to gain by what I did. The most I would have gotten out of the raid—besides the excitement—was a bunch of spinach which I don't like. If I had been home at the right time, at the dinner hour, I could have had everything I could have stolen from that fruit stand and it would have all been clean and fresh and well cooked. I also would have escaped the licking I got when I landed home after midnight.

The same thing applies all along the line. You'll find you're much surer of getting whatever you want —and of getting it with less grief—if you'll go after it in a decent, intelligent way. The quicker you learn this the luckier you are. I know I'm right, I have some pretty concrete examples to prove it. . . .

A lot of my old buddies from my old neighborhood, which wasn't exactly an ideal place for kids to grow up, didn't "smarten up," continued to go after things the wrong way. They haven't fared too well. As those buddies of mine became older their motives naturally became more violent and they naturally went out for bigger things. And it all caught up with them. Some of them landed in reform school. One went to jail. I was lucky. I found out in time.

Also, let me tell you, I can't see anything wrong about kids ganging up and wearing special clothes and talking a special way; like you bobby-sockers do. In time of war the kids who're just under the fighting age always do this. I'm not going to sound off or try to be profound— but the best psychologists explain it's because you who are too young to fight or go to work in a defense plant feel unimportant and maybe a little insecure that you band together with your own kind of clothes and your own kind of lingo. During the last war the kids who did this—and wore pork pie hats and raglan coats and floppy galoshes and flowing hair and injected a lot of new words and phrases into our good old language —were called Finalehoppers. They liked to stick around until the last dance too. It's too bad some of the parents who wring their hands over the bobby-sockers today forget what they did under similar conditions.

As soon as the last war was over, you'll be interested to hear, the Finalehoppers, grown a couple of years older, quit herding together. Just as I believe you bobby-sockers will. . . .

"DEAR Frankie," you write me . . . Then you go on your own way. One who must be nameless writes: "My sisters continually wear clothes I just washed, took out of the cleaners or bought. I have gotten so exhausted from this that I have quit my job in a five and dime store. Besides never taking me anywhere with them my sisters always say I am trying to get out of a piece of housecleaning when I study. And if I put my book down they say I'm a martyr. My mother will not tell them to stop. I can't cry any more as my tears are all gone. But I can't stand this any more. . . ."

Another letter says: "It seems my mother doesn't want me at all. It's my older (Continued on page 110)

**STILL FROM 'IT HAPPENED IN BROOKLYN'
(1947)**
This serious romance has Sinatra as a returning war
veteran with Gloria Grahame as a Navy nurse. /
In diesem Liebesdrama spielt Sinatra einen Kriegs-
veteranen und Gloria Grahame eine Marinekranken-
schwester. / Dans ce drame sentimental, Sinatra joue le
rôle d'un vétéran qui revient de la guerre et Gloria
Grahame celui d'une infirmière dans l'armée.

**STILL FROM 'IT HAPPENED IN BROOKLYN'
(1947)**
With Jimmy Durante, a stage performer from the
previous generation who crossed over to movies
when talkies began. / Mit Jimmy Durante, einem
Bühnenstar der vorhergehenden Generation, der mit
der Einführung des Tonfilms zum Kino wechselte. /
En compagnie de Jimmy Durante, ancien acteur de
théâtre venu au cinéma avec les films parlants.

**STILL FROM 'THE MIRACLE OF THE BELLS'
(1948)**
In his first non-musical role, ex-choirboy Sinatra plays a
provincial priest. One woman even knelt to kiss his ring,
thinking he was a real priest. / In seiner ersten nicht-
musikalischen Rolle spielt der ehemalige Chorknabe
Sinatra einen Priester in der Provinz. Eine Frau kniete
sogar vor ihm nieder, um seinen Ring zu küssen, weil sie
ihn für einen echten Geistlichen hielt. / Dans ce premier
rôle uniquement parlé, l'ancien enfant de chœur Sinatra
incarne un prêtre. Il est si naturel dans son rôle qu'un
jour une femme a baisé sa bague, persuadée qu'il était
un authentique prélat.

**ON THE SET OF 'THE MIRACLE OF THE
BELLS' (1948)**
An off-camera moment with co-star Fred MacMurray
and the snappily-dressed assistant director. / Ein
Schnappschuss während der Dreharbeiten mit Kollege
Fred MacMurray und einem fesch gekleideten
Regieassistenten. / Loin de la caméra, en compagnie
de Fred MacMurray, son partenaire à l'écran, et de
l'assistant du réalisateur dans une tenue tapageuse.

"I'm supposed to have a Ph.D. on the subject of women. But the truth is I've flunked more often than not. I'm very fond of women; I admire them. But, like all men, I don't understand them."
Frank Sinatra

„Man sagt mir ja nach, dass ich im Fach Frauen-kunde promoviert habe, aber in Wirklichkeit bin ich öfter durch die Prüfung gefallen, als ich sie bestanden habe. Ich mag Frauen, ich bewundere sie, aber wie alle Männer kann ich sie einfach nicht verstehen."
Frank Sinatra

« Il paraît que je sais tout sur les femmes. C'est faux : je me suis gouré bien des fois. Les femmes ? Je les aime, je les admire, mais comme tous les hommes, je ne les comprends pas. »
Frank Sinatra

PORTRAIT FOR 'THE KISSING BANDIT' (1948)
Sinatra with frequent MGM co-star Kathryn Grayson. He considered this his worst film and it became a running gag in his family. / Sinatra mit Kathryn Grayson, die häufig in MGM-Filmen mitspielte. Er hielt diesen für seinen schlechtesten Film, und das wurde zu einer Art „running gag" in seiner Familie. / Sinatra aux côtés de Kathryn Grayson, qui fut souvent sa partenaire dans les films de la MGM. Frank considérait que c'était son plus mauvais film, et il en plaisantait souvent en famille.

STILL FROM 'TAKE ME OUT TO THE BALL GAME' (1949)
Kelly and Sinatra are baseball players fighting for the romantic affections of Esther Williams, the new owner of the team. / Kelly und Sinatra als Baseballspieler, die um die Gunst von K. C. (Esther Williams), der neuen Eigentümerin der Mannschaft, buhlen. / Kelly et Sinatra incarnent deux joueurs de base-ball qui se disputent les faveurs de la belle Esther Williams, devenue propriétaire de l'équipe.

"Frank's a hell of a guy. He tries to live his own life. If he could only stay away from the broads and devote some time to develop himself as an actor, he'd be one of the best in the business."
Humphrey Bogart

„Frank ist ein toller Kerl. Er versucht, sein eigenes Leben zu leben. Wenn er die Finger von den Frauen lassen könnte und ein bisschen Zeit in seine Weiterentwicklung als Schauspieler steckte, dann wäre er einer der Besten in diesem Geschäft."
Humphrey Bogart

« Frank est un type étonnant. Il veut mener sa vie comme il l'entend, mais s'il en faisait un peu moins pour les femmes et un peu plus pour le métier, il deviendrait un grand, un très grand acteur. »
Humphrey Bogart

STILL FROM 'TAKE ME OUT TO THE BALL GAME' (1949)
Sinatra is worn out, and Kelly is being pressured to fix the games by some unsavory gamblers. / Ryan (Sinatra) ist am Ende, aber O'Brien (Kelly) wird von zwielichtigen Wettbetrügern unter Druck gesetzt, die Spiele zu manipulieren. / Sinatra est épuisé et des parieurs sans scrupules font pression sur Kelly pour qu'il truque les matchs.

PAGES 46/47
STILL FROM 'TAKE ME OUT TO THE BALL GAME' (1949)
Sinatra and Kelly are dancers on the vaudeville circuit who are more successful playing baseball. / Sinatra und Kelly spielen Varietétänzer, die allerdings mehr Erfolg als Baseballspieler haben. / Sinatra et Kelly ont moins de succès en danseurs de music-hall qu'en joueurs de base-ball.

STILL FROM 'ON THE TOWN' (1949)
Sinatra and Kelly (with co-star Jules Munshin) are back
in sailor suits and have 24 hours on the town. / Sinatra
und Kelly (mit Kollege Jules Munshin) stecken wieder in
ihren Matrosenanzügen und haben 24 Stunden Zeit,
New York unsicher zu machen. / Sinatra et Kelly (ainsi
que l'acteur Jules Munshin) ont rendossé l'uniforme de
la marine ; les voici en permission pour vingt-quatre
heures.

*"Throughout my career, if I have done anything,
I have paid attention to every note and every word
I sing – if I respect the song. If I cannot project this
to a listener, I fail."*
Frank Sinatra

*„Wenn ich während meiner ganzen Karriere etwas
getan habe, dann war es, auf jede Note zu achten,
die ich singe und auf jedes Wort – weil ich Achtung
vor dem Lied habe. Wenn ich das dem Zuhörer
nicht vermitteln kann, dann habe ich versagt."*
Frank Sinatra

STILL FROM 'ON THE TOWN' (1949)
Spontaneous performances in front of actual New York landmarks gave the film a spark that resulted in a box-office hit. / Spontane Einlagen vor echten New Yorker Wahrzeichen (hier die Rockefeller Plaza) gaben dem Film einen besonderen Reiz, der sich auch im Kassen-erfolg niederschlug. / C'est aux scènes de rues devant des sites marquants de la ville de New York que ce film doit son mordant et son succès commercial.

« Tout au long de ma carrière, je me suis appliqué à respecter chaque note et chaque parole des chansons que j'ai interprétées, du moins celles qui en valaient la peine. Et si le public ne l'a pas senti, c'est que je n'ai pas su m'y prendre. »
Frank Sinatra

STILL FROM 'ON THE TOWN' (1949)
Even the stagebound numbers, such as this duo with
Betty Garrett, benefited from MGM's high-end art
direction. / Selbst die Studionummern — wie dieses
Duett mit Betty Garrett — profitierten von der
hochwertigen Ausstattung des MGM-Films. / Même
les numéros tournés en studio, comme ce duo avec
Betty Garrett, prennent une nouvelle dimension
lorsqu'ils sont dirigés avec le professionnalisme de
la MGM.

PORTRAIT FOR 'ON THE TOWN' (1949)
Besides performing in some outlandish moments, Gene
Kelly (right) received his first co-directing credit with
Stanley Donen. / Gene Kelly (rechts) durfte nicht nur in
einigen recht ausgefallenen Kostümen auftreten,
sondern wurde erstmals auch neben Stanley Donen als
Koregisseur genannt. / Non content de jouer dans des
scènes époustouflantes, Gene Kelly (à droite, aux côtés
de Sinatra) est pour la première fois mentionné comme
coréalisateur avec Stanley Donen.

STILL FROM 'DOUBLE DYNAMITE' (1951)
Dropped by MGM and his agency, Sinatra recovered
from vocal problems and became a freelance actor. /
Nachdem ihn MGM und seine Agentur fallengelassen
hatten, erholte sich Sinatra von seinen Stimmband-
problemen und wurde freiberuflicher Schauspieler. /
Abandonné par la MGM et par son agence, Sinatra, une
fois ses cordes vocales guéries, devient un acteur
indépendant.

PAGES 52/53
PORTRAIT FOR 'ON THE TOWN' (1949)
Kelly choreographed the dance numbers with his
characteristic high energy. As usual, Sinatra never
went to rehearsals but was always prepared. / Kelly
choreographierte die Tanzeinlagen mit seiner typischen
Energie. Wie üblich erschien Sinatra nie zu den Proben,
war aber stets vorbereitet. / C'est Kelly qui a
chorégraphié les numéros de danse avec son habituelle
énergie. Fidèle à lui-même, Sinatra n'a assisté à aucune
répétition mais s'est tenu prêt le moment venu.

STILL FROM 'DOUBLE DYNAMITE' (1951)
In this non-musical comedy Sinatra plays a bank teller suspected of embezzling, and straight man to Groucho Marx. RKO owner Howard Hughes shelved the film because it was so bad. / In diesem Lustspiel ohne Musik spielt Sinatra nicht nur einen Bankangestellten, den man verdächtigt, Geld unterschlagen zu haben, sondern gibt auch noch den „straight man" für Groucho Marx. RKO-Besitzer Howard Hughes fand den Film aber so schlecht, dass er ihn ganz schnell auf Eis legte. / Dans cette comédie sans chansons, Sinatra joue le rôle d'un employé de banque soupçonné d'escroquerie. Il sert de faire-valoir à Groucho Marx. Le propriétaire de la RKO, Howard Hughes, mit le film de côté en raison de ses piètres qualités.

"What Sinatra has is beyond talent. It's some sort of magnetism that goes in higher revolutions than that of anybody else, anybody in the whole of show business."
Billy Wilder, writer/producer/director

„Was Sinatra besitzt, ist mehr als Talent. Es ist eine Art Anziehungskraft, die stärker ist als die irgendeiner anderen Person im gesamten Showgeschäft."
Billy Wilder, Drehbuchautor/Produzent/Regisseur

« Sinatra possède autre chose que du talent, une sorte de magnétisme qui dépasse largement celui de toutes les vedettes du show-biz sans exception. »
Billy Wilder, scénariste/producteur/réalisateur

STILL FROM 'MEET DANNY WILSON' (1952)
In his first performance as solo male star and title
character, Sinatra is a part-time lounge singer and pool
hustler. / In seiner ersten Rolle als einziger männlicher
Star und Titelheld eines Films hat Sinatra einen
Teilzeitjob als Clubsänger und spielt nebenbei auch
noch Poolbillard. / Pour la première fois, Sinatra est la
vedette du film avec ce rôle-titre ; son personnage est à
la fois chanteur de bar et joueur de billard.

STILL FROM 'MEET DANNY WILSON' (1952)
Although Danny has lighter moments opposite Shelley
Winters, the plot takes a serious turn after the character
achieves success. / Obwohl es auch ein paar heitere
Szenen mit Sinatra an der Seite von Shelley Winters
gibt, nimmt die Handlung eine Wende zum Ernsthaften,
nachdem Danny berufliche Erfolge erzielt. / Malgré
quelques scènes frivoles entre Danny et Shelley
Winters, l'intrigue prend de l'épaisseur dès que le
personnage connaît le succès.

STILL FROM 'MEET DANNY WILSON' (1952)
Still a teen idol, but looking a lot older than in the photo
held by a young fan. In reality, Sinatra's career was so
low he had to borrow money to visit Ava Gardner on
location. / Danny ist noch immer ein Teenageridol, aber
er sieht schon viel älter aus als auf dem Foto, das die
junge Verehrerin in Händen hält. In Wirklichkeit hatte
Sinatras Karriere zu dieser Zeit einen solchen Tiefpunkt
erreicht, dass er sich Geld borgen musste, um Ava
Gardner bei Dreharbeiten besuchen zu können. /
Même s'il reste l'idole des adolescents, Sinatra n'est plus
aussi jeune que sur la photo exhibée par cette jeune
admiratrice. Dans la réalité sa carrière est au point mort
et il est contraint d'emprunter de l'argent pour rendre
visite à Ava Gardner sur le lieu du tournage.

"There are moments when it's too quiet,
particularly late at night or early in the mornings.
That's when you know there's something lacking in
your life."
Frank Sinatra

STILL FROM 'MEET DANNY WILSON' (1952)
Danny is caught in the clutches of a manager involved
with racketeers, an ironic foreshadowing of real issues
in Sinatra's later career. / Danny steckt in den Fängen
eines Managers, der sich mit zwielichtigen Gestalten
eingelassen hat – eine ironische Vorausdeutung dessen,
was in Sinatras späterer Karriere tatsächlich immer
wieder ein Thema war. / Danny est entre les griffes d'un
manager qui magouille avec des racketteurs – sorte de
présage ironique des ennuis qui arriveront à Sinatra
dans la phase finale de sa carrière.

„Es gibt Augenblicke, in denen es zu still ist,
insbesondere spät in der Nacht oder am frühen
Morgen. Dann spürst du, dass etwas in deinem
Leben fehlt."
Frank Sinatra

« Tard le soir ou tôt le matin, il arrive que le silence
devienne pesant. C'est là que vous prenez
conscience qu'il vous manque quelque chose dans
la vie. »
Frank Sinatra

**STILL FROM 'FROM HERE TO ETERNITY'
(1953)**
Sinatra had a legendary struggle to overcome the
objections of studio chief Harry Cohn for the part of
Angelo Maggio. In the end Sinatra got the part because
Eli Wallach dropped out to do a play. / Wie hart Sinatra
gegen die Einwände von Studioboss Harry Cohn
ankämpfen musste, um die Rolle des Angelo Maggio
spielen zu dürfen, ist bereits Legende. Am Ende erhielt
Sinatra die Rolle, weil Eli Wallach wegen eines
Bühnenstücks absprang. / Sinatra a dû se battre pour
obtenir le rôle d'Angelo Maggio contre l'avis de Harry
Cohn, le directeur des studios. Finalement, la défection
d'Eli Wallach, appelé pour une jouer une pièce, a porté
chance à l'acteur.

"Only my friends can call me a little wop."
Angelo Maggio, 'From Here to Eternity' (1953)

„Nur meine Freunde dürfen mich ‚kleiner
Spaghettifresser' nennen."
Angelo Maggio, Verdammt in alle Ewigkeit (1953)

« Personne n'a le droit de me traiter de petit Rital,
sauf mes amis. »
Angelo Maggio, Tant qu'il y aura des hommes (1953)

ON THE SET OF 'FROM HERE TO ETERNITY' (1953)

With co-star Montgomery Clift and director Fred Zinnemann. Sinatra worked privately, reading and rereading his script until he understood every nuance of it – just like he learned songs – so that his unrehearsed performance was spontaneous. / Mit Kollege Montgomery Clift und Regisseur Fred Zinnemann. Sinatra arbeitete für sich und las das Drehbuch immer wieder, bis er jede Nuance verstanden hatte – genau so, wie er seine Lieder lernte –, damit seine ungeprobte Darstellung spontan wirkte. / En compagnie de son partenaire à l'écran Montgomery Clift et du réalisateur Fred Zinnemann. Sinatra travaille avec autant d'ardeur que pour apprendre une chanson. Il lit et relit son rôle jusqu'à en saisir chaque nuance, si bien que son jeu en devient complètement naturel.

STILL FROM 'FROM HERE TO ETERNITY' (1953)
Sgt. Warden (Burt Lancaster, center) intevenes in a
confrontation between Maggio and sadistic Sgt. Judson
(Ernest Borgnine, left). / Sergeant Warden (Burt
Lancaster, Mitte) schreitet bei einer Konfrontation
zwischen Maggio und dem sadistischen Unteroffizier
Judson (Ernest Borgnine, links) ein. / Le sergent
Warden (Burt Lancaster, au centre) intervient lors d'une
confrontation entre Maggio et ce sadique de Sergent
Judson (Ernest Borgnine, à gauche)

STILL FROM 'FROM HERE TO ETERNITY' (1953)
Sinatra's effortless naturalistic performance as the
combative Italian-American earned him a supporting
actor Academy Award. / Für seine natürlich wirkende
Leistung als kämpferischer Italoamerikaner erhielt
Sinatra einen „Oscar" als bester Nebendarsteller. /
Fluide et naturel, le jeu de Sinatra en Italo-Américain
combatif lui vaut l'oscar du Meilleur second rôle.

PAGES 64/65
STILL FROM 'FROM HERE TO ETERNITY' (1953)
For a drunk scene Montgomery Clift got drunk, so
Sinatra sobered him up with coffee so that he could
play drunk. / Sinatra musste M. Clift erst einmal mit
Kaffee wieder nüchtern machen, damit dieser den
Betrunkenen auch wirklich spielen konnte. / Sinatra a
fait boire du café à M. Clift pour que ce dernier,
réellement ivre, pût jouer sa scène : un homme ... saoûl.

STILL FROM 'SUDDENLY' (1954)
With newly-won Oscar-certification as a dramatic
actor Sinatra had the confidence to portray an outright
villain. / Der frischverliehene Schauspiel-„Oscar" gab
Sinatra das nötige Selbstbewusstsein, um einen
richtigen Bösewicht zu spielen. / Sinatra, qui venait
d'obtenir un oscar dans un rôle dramatique, se sentait
de taille à interpréter le rôle d'un véritable malfaiteur.

STILL FROM 'SUDDENLY' (1954)
In this independently produced film noir, Sinatra's
character manhandles a woman and strikes a child. /
In diesem unabhängig produzierten Film noir
misshandelt Sinatra in seiner Rolle eine Frau und
schlägt ein Kind. / Dans ce film noir, produit par un
indépendant, le personnage qu'incarne Sinatra
malmène une femme et frappe un enfant.

STILL FROM 'SUDDENLY' (1954)
Would-be presidential assassin John Baron holds the
local sheriff (Sterling Hayden) hostage. / Vor seinem
Attentat auf den Präsidenten nimmt John Baron
(Sinatra) den örtlichen Sheriff (Sterling Hayden) als
Geisel. / John Baron, le futur assassin du président,
prend en otage le shérif incarné par Sterling Hayden.

"The thing about killing you or her or him is that
I wouldn't be getting paid for it and I don't like
giving anything away for free."
John Baron, 'Suddenly' (1954)

„Das Problem, wenn ich dich oder sie oder ihn
umlege, ist, dass ich dafür nicht bezahlt werde.
Und ich geb nicht gerne was umsonst."
John Baron, *Der Attentäter* (1954)

STILL FROM 'SUDDENLY' (1954)
Ultimately Baron dies (another first for a Sinatra role) as
violently as he lived. / Am Ende stirbt Baron (auch
etwas Neues für eine Sinatra-Rolle) ebenso gewaltsam
wie er gelebt hatte. / La vie de John Baron a été
particulièrement violente ; sa mort le sera également
(une première dans la carrière cinématographique de
Sinatra).

*« Moi je veux bien tuer n'importe qui — toi, lui, elle,
sauf que ça ne me rapporterait pas un rond, et le
bénévolat, c'est pas mon truc. »*
John Baron, *Je dois tuer* (1954)

"Basically, I'm for anything that gets you through the night, be it prayer, tranquilizers, or a bottle of Jack Daniels."
Frank Sinatra

„Im Grunde bin ich für alles, was einen durch die Nacht bringt, ob es ein Gebet ist, ein Beruhigungs- mittel oder eine Flasche Jack Daniels."
Frank Sinatra

« À vrai dire, tout ce qui vous aide à venir à bout de la nuit est bon à prendre : une prière, un somnifère ou une bouteille de Jack Daniels. »
Frank Sinatra

STILL FROM 'YOUNG AT HEART' (1954)
Sinatra's first project at Warner Bros. was a return to drama with a musical context. He sings 'One for My Baby' and 'Someone to Watch Over Me' among others. / Sinatras erster Film für Warner Bros. war eine Rückkehr zum Drama in einem musikalischen Kontext. Er singt unter anderem „One for My Baby" und „Someone to Watch Over Me". / Les débuts de Sinatra à la Warner Bros. ont été marqués par un retour à l'alliance du cinéma et de la musique. Entre autres chansons, il interprète « One for My Baby » et « Someone to Watch Over Me ».

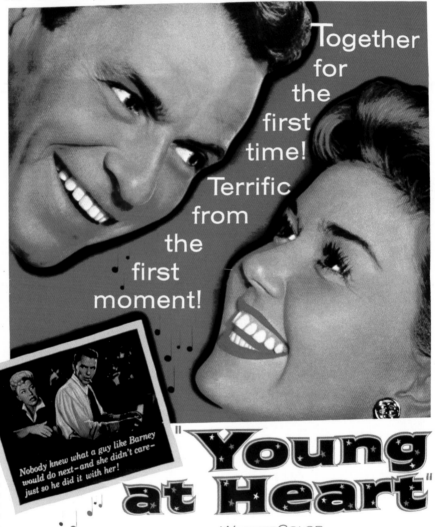

WARNER BROS. PRESENT

DORIS DAY AND
FRANK SINATRA!

Together for the first time! Terrific from the first moment!

Nobody knew what a guy like Barney would do next—and she didn't care— just so he did it with her!

"Young at Heart"

COLOR BY WARNERCOLOR

WARNER BROS.' HEART-SINGING STORY WITH ALL THAT'S SO SWELL ABOUT DORIS DAY AND ALL THAT'S SO SPECIAL ABOUT FRANK SINATRA!

GIG YOUNG ETHEL BARRYMORE DOROTHY MALONE

STILL FROM 'YOUNG AT HEART' (1954)
Sinatra plays a penniless composer who falls for one
of four daughters, played by Doris Day. It was the first
of five features with director Gordon Douglas. /
Sinatra spielt einen abgebrannten Komponisten, der
sich in eine von vier Schwestern verliebt, die von Doris
Day gespielt wird. Für Sinatra war es der erste von fünf
Spielfilmen unter der Regie von Gordon Douglas. /
Sinatra interprète un compositeur fauché amoureux
d'une jeune fille (Doris Day) qui a trois sœurs ; ce fut le
premier de cinq rôles dirigés par le réalisateur Gordon
Douglas.

POSTER FOR 'YOUNG AT HEART' (1954)

STILL FROM 'NOT AS A STRANGER' (1955)
Sinatra accepted a supporting role in this social
melodrama by producer/director Stanley Kramer. /
Sinatra nahm eine Nebenrolle in dem Gesellschafts-
melodram unter der Regie von Stanley Kramer an,
der den Film auch produzierte. / Sinatra a accepté un
second rôle dans un mélodrame social mis en scène par
Stanley Kramer.

STILL FROM 'NOT AS A STRANGER' (1955)
Sinatra is a face in the crowd sandwiched between Lee
Marvin and top-billed Robert Mitchum. / Sinatra ist ein
Gesicht in der Menge zwischen Lee Marvin und Robert
Mitchum, der die Hauptrolle spielte. / Visage parmi la
foule, Sinatra est encadré par Lee Marvin et la vedette
du film, Robert Mitchum.

STILL FROM 'GUYS AND DOLLS' (1955)
Sinatra returns to his musical roots in the film
adaptation of the stage play based on Damon Runyon's
characters. He also made the best-ever recording of
'Luck Be a Lady.' / Sinatra kehrte zu seinen
musikalischen Wurzeln zurück in der Verfilmung des
Bühnenstücks nach Charakteren von Damon Runyon.
Er machte auch die beste Aufnahme aller Zeiten von
„Luck Be a Lady". / Sinatra revient à ses racines dans
l'adaptation cinématographique d'une comédie
musicale qui met en scène les personnages de Damon
Runyon. À cette occasion, il fait le meilleur
enregistrement jamais réalisé de « Luck Be a Lady ».

*"The streets are covered with tourists and I do not
want you molested."*
Nathan Detroit, 'Guy and Dolls' (1955)

*„Die Straßen sind voller Touristen, und ich möchte
nicht, dass du belästigt wirst."*
Nathan Detroit, *Schwere Jungen, leichte Mädchen* (1955)

*« Les rues sont infestées de touristes, et je ne
voudrais pas que tu te fasses agresser. »*
Nathan Detroit, *Blanches colombes et vilains messieurs*
(1955)

STILL FROM 'GUYS AND DOLLS' (1955)
Frank thought that the film was miscast, and that he
should have played Marlon Brando's role. Sinatra also
lost out to Brando for the part of Terry Malloy in 'On
the Waterfront.' / Frank war der Meinung, dass der Film
fehlbesetzt war, und dass er Marlon Brandos Rolle hätte
spielen sollen. Sinatra verlor auch die Rolle des Terry
Malloy in *Die Faust im Nacken* an Brando. / Bien que
convaincu qu'il y a une erreur de casting et que le rôle
de Marlon Brando aurait dû lui revenir, Sinatra devra
également lui abandonner le rôle de Terry Malloy dans
le film *Sur les quais.*

PAGES 78/79
ON THE SET OF 'GUYS AND DOLLS' (1955)
Michael Kidd's choreography was less demanding for
the almost 40-year-old Sinatra than Gene Kelly's. /
Michael Kidds Choreographie war für den fast
vierzigjährigen Sinatra weniger anstrengend als die von
Gene Kelly. / Pour Sinatra, qui approche de la
quarantaine, la chorégraphie de Michael Kid est moins
exigeante que celle de Kelly.

STILL FROM 'THE TENDER TRAP' (1955)
Sinatra was not afraid to be cast as a womanizer who falls for ingenue Debbie Reynolds. Frank gave the film title as a challenge to songwriters Sammy Cahn and Jimmy Van Heusen, who delivered in 40 minutes. / Sinatra hatte keine Angst davor, die Rolle des Schürzenjägers zu spielen, der sich in die naive Julie (Debbie Reynolds) verliebt. Frank gab den Textern Sammy Cahn und Jimmy Van Heusen den Titel des Films als Liedtitel vor, und in 40 Minuten stand der gleichnamige Song. / Sinatra ne craint pas d'être filmé en dragueur enamouré de la jeune ingénue Debbie Reynolds. L'acteur avait soumis le titre du film aux paroliers Sammy Cahn et Jimmy Van Heusen ; 40 minutes plus tard, ils en avaient composé une chanson.

"Oh, God, Frank Sinatra could be the sweetest, most charming man in the world when he was in the mood."
Ava Gardner, second wife

„O Gott, Frank Sinatra konnte der liebenswürdigste, charmanteste Mann auf der Welt sein, wenn er entsprechend aufgelegt war."
Ava Gardner, zweite Ehefrau

STILL FROM 'THE TENDER TRAP' (1955)
The shrug, a signature Sinatra reaction, in a scene with
Reynolds and co-stars Celeste Holm and David Wayne. /
Das Schulterzucken, eine typische Sinatra-Geste, in
einer Szene mit Reynolds, Celeste Holm und David
Wayne. / Dans cette scène avec Reynolds, et les acteurs
Celeste Holms et David Wayne, Sinatra hausse les
épaules — un geste qui le caractérise.

« Quand il était dans un bon jour, Frank Sinatra
pouvait être le plus agréable, le plus charmant des
hommes. »
Ava Gardner, sa deuxième épouse

STILL FROM 'THE MAN WITH THE GOLDEN ARM' (1955)
The portrayal of a troubled addict got Sinatra his second (and last) Academy Award nomination as an actor. / Für die Darstellung eines Drogenabhängigen in Schwierigkeiten wurde Sinatra zum zweiten (und letzten) Mal als Schauspieler für einen Academy Award nominiert. / Ce portrait d'un drogué tourmenté vaut à Sinatra sa seconde et dernière nomination aux Oscars en tant qu'acteur.

PORTRAIT FOR 'THE MAN WITH THE GOLDEN ARM' (1955)
Sinatra, shown with co-star Kim Novak, was sent the script at the same time as Marlon Brando. Frank said "yes" the next day before Brando could reply. / Sinatra, hier mit seiner Kollegin Kim Novak, erhielt das Drehbuch zur gleichen Zeit wie Marlon Brando. Frank sagte bereits am folgenden Tag zu, bevor Brando reagieren konnte. / Sinatra, ici avec sa partenaire Kim Novak, reçoit le scénario en même temps que Marlon Brando. Frank donna son accord dès le lendemain, avant que Brando ait eu le temps de répondre.

PAGES 84/85
ON THE SET OF 'THE MAN WITH THE GOLDEN ARM' (1955)
Sinatra's 'golden arm' deals winning hands during illegal card games. Here director Otto Preminger (left) and novelist Nelson Algren (center) sit in on a hand. / Frankies „goldener Arm" teilt ein siegreiches Blatt bei illegalen Kartenspielen aus. Hier schauen ihm Regisseur Otto Preminger (links) und Romanautor Nelson Algren (Mitte) über die Schulter. / Le « bras d'or » qu'interprète Sinatra distribue des cartes gagnantes lors de parties illégales. Ici le réalisateur Otto Preminger (à gauche) et le romancier Nelson Algren (au centre) assistent à une manche.

STILL FROM 'THE MAN WITH THE GOLDEN ARM' (1955)
Desperate for a fix after losing a big game, Sinatra rifles the drug-dealer's room as best friend Arnold Strang tries to calm him down. / Nachdem er ein großes Spiel verloren hat, durchwühlt Frankie auf der verzweifelten Suche nach einem Schuss das Zimmer des Drogen-dealers, während ihn sein bester Freund (Arnold Strang) zu beruhigen versucht. / Sinatra vient de perdre une grosse partie et il a désespérément besoin d'un shoot ; il fouille la chambre d'un dealer tandis que son meilleur ami, Arnold Strang, tente de le calmer.

STILL FROM 'THE MAN WITH THE GOLDEN ARM' (1955)
Wanted for a murder he didn't commit, Sinatra becomes violent towards Kim Novak as he goes cold turkey before handing himself in to the police. / Frankie, der wegen eines Mordes, den er nicht begangen hat, gesucht wird, zeigt sich – nachdem er seine Drogen abrupt abgesetzt hat – Kim Novak gegenüber gewalttätig, und stellt sich anschließend der Polizei. / Recherché pour un meurtre qu'il n'a pas commis, Sinatra brutalise Kim Novak, puis entreprend un sevrage brutal avant de se rendre à la police.

"I'm the kind of guy, boy, when I move, watch my smoke."
Frankie Machine, 'The Man with the Golden Arm' (1955)

„Ich bin ein Typ, wenn der sich bewegt, Junge, dann staubt's!"
Frankie Machine, *Der Mann mit dem goldenen Arm* (1955)

« Moi, je suis comme ça, quand je me déplace, mieux vaut regarder de quel côté va la vapeur. »
Frankie Machine, *L'Homme au bras d'or* (1955)

STILL FROM 'HIGH SOCIETY' (1956)
Sinatra as tabloid reporter Mike Connor, sings 'Who
Wants to Be a Millionaire?' with Celeste Holm. / Sinatra
singt als Klatschreporter Mike Connor „Who Wants to
Be a Millionaire?" mit Celeste Holm. / Dans le rôle de
Mike Connor, reporter pour un tabloïde, Sinatra
interprète « Who Wants to Be a Millionaire ? » aux côtés
de Celeste Holm.

ON THE SET OF 'HIGH SOCIETY' (1956)
Rehearsing 'You're Sensational' with director Charles
Walters and non-singing co-star Grace Kelly. / Bei den
Proben zu "You're Sensational" mit Regisseur Charles
Walters und seiner gesanglosen Kollegin Grace Kelly. /
Sinatra répète « You're sensational » sous la houlette du
réalisateur Charles Walters et de sa partenaire, Grace
Kelly qui, elle, ne chante pas.

STILL FROM 'HIGH SOCIETY' (1956)

Although he had shared a stage with Bing Crosby, this was Sinatra's first movie with the crooner who had inspired his style. Here they sing 'Well, Did You Evah?' / Obwohl er bereits mit Bing Crosby auf der Bühne gestanden hatte, war dies sein erster Film mit dem Sänger, der seinen eigenen Stil maßgeblich beeinflusst hatte. Hier singen sie „Well, Did You Evah?" im Duett. / Sinatra s'est déjà produit avec Bing Crosby, mais c'est ici son premier film avec le crooner qui a tant influencé son style. Ici, ils interprètent « Well, Did You Evah ».

STILL FROM 'HIGH SOCIETY' (1956)
The Sinatra/Crosby approach was a bit different than James Stewart and Cary Grant in the original 'Philadelphia Story.' / Sinatra und Crosby spielten ihre Rollen ein wenig anders als James Stewart und Cary Grant im Originalfilm *Die Nacht vor der Hochzeit*. / L'interprétation de Sinatra et Crosby diffère quelque peu de celle de James Stewart et Cary Grant dans la version originale d'*Indiscrétions*.

STILL FROM 'HIGH SOCIETY' (1956)
Grace Kelly found all the inspiration she needed in
Katharine Hepburn's earlier portrayal of Tracy Lord. /
Grace Kelly fand alle Inspiration, die sie benötigte, in
Katharine Hepburns früherer Darstellung der Tracy
Lord. / Grace Kelly trouve toute l'inspiration nécessaire
dans l'interprétation que Katharine Hepburn avait
donnée du personnage de Tracy Lord.

STILL FROM 'HIGH SOCIETY' (1956)
Cole Porter received a staggering $250,000 for the
use of 9 of his songs in the film. / Cole Porter erhielt
schwindelerregende $250.000 dafür, dass neun seiner
Lieder im Film verwendet wurden. / Cole Porter
empocha une somme faramineuse — 250 000 dollars ! —
pour les droits d'utilisation de neuf de ses chansons
dans le film.

STILL FROM 'HIGH SOCIETY' (1956)
Self-conscious about rehearsing in front of his hero Bing Crosby, Sinatra would join him on the set just before a take. / Weil er zu gehemmt war, vor seinem Idol Bing Crosby zu proben, trat Sinatra immer erst kurz vor der eigentlichen Aufnahme zu ihm hinaus. / Gêné de répéter devant son héros Bing Crosby, Sinatra le rejoignait sur le plateau juste avant les prises de vue.

STILL FROM 'HIGH SOCIETY' (1956)
Sinatra never attempted to match Stewart's physical presence – he was the same height and weight as Kelly. / Sinatra versuchte nie, Stewarts körperliche Präsenz zu imitieren – er war genauso groß und schwer wie Kelly. / Sinatra ne tente même pas d'égaler la présence physique de Stewart – il faisait la même taille et le même poids que Kelly.

STILL FROM 'AROUND THE WORLD IN EIGHTY DAYS' (1956)
Sinatra made many cameo appearances in his career including this one with Cantinflas, David Niven and Marlene Dietrich. / Sinatra hatte in seiner langen Karriere zahlreiche Cameo-Auftritte, darunter auch diesen mit Cantinflas, David Niven und Marlene Dietrich. / Au cours de sa carrière, Sinatra fit souvent de brèves apparitions dans des films comme ici en compagnie de Cantinflas, David Niven et Marlene Dietrich.

STILL FROM 'JOHNNY CONCHO' (1956)
Despite his added role as producer, Sinatra seems as uncomfortable in his first western as he was for 'The Kissing Bandit.' / Obwohl er den Film auch produzierte, schien sich Sinatra in seinem ersten Western ebenso unwohl zu fühlen wie in *Ein Bandit zum Küssen*. / Bien qu'il soit également le producteur du film, Sinatra paraît tout aussi mal à l'aise dans son premier western que dans *Le Bandit amoureux*.

ON THE SET OF 'THE PRIDE AND THE PASSION' (1957)

Sinatra and director Stanley Kramer (pointing) were reunited in a more epic endeavor than their first picture 'Not as a Stranger.' / Sinatra und Regisseur Stanley Kramer (mit ausgestrecktem Arm) arbeiteten bei diesem im Vergleich zu ... *und nicht als ein Fremder* etwas epischer angelegten Film wieder zusammen. / Frank Sinatra et le réalisateur Stanley Kramer se retrouvent pour le tournage de cette fresque épique, un registre bien différent de leur premier long métrage, *Pour que vivent les hommes.*

"Nothing anybody's said or written about me ever bothers me, except when it does."
Frank Sinatra

„Nichts, was irgendjemand über mich gesagt oder geschrieben hat, macht mir je etwas aus — außer wenn es mir etwas ausmacht."
Frank Sinatra

« On peut dire de moi ou écrire sur moi tout ce qu'on veut. En règle générale, je m'en balance. Mais il y a des limites. »
Frank Sinatra

**STILL FROM 'THE PRIDE AND THE PASSION'
(1957)**
Shoemaker Frank Sinatra and girlfriend Sophia Loren
lead a group of guerilla fighters as they haul a giant
cannon across Spain so that it can be used to defeat the
French invaders. / Schuster Miguel (Frank Sinatra) und
seine Freundin (Sophia Loren) führen eine Gruppe von
Partisanen an, die eine riesige Kanone quer durch
Spanien schleppt, damit sie im Kampf gegen die
französischen Eindringlinge eingesetzt werden kann. /
Le cordonnier Frank Sinatra et Sophia Loren, sa bien-
aimée, sont à la tête d'un groupe de guérilleros. Ils
traversent l'Espagne avec un gros canon destiné à
repousser l'envahisseur français.

STILL FROM 'THE PRIDE AND THE PASSION'
(1957)
British officer Cary Grant helps the Spaniards to
repair and operate the cannon. / Als britischer Offizier
hilft Cary Grant den Spaniern, mit den Kanonen zu
hantieren. / L'officier britannique Cary Grant aide les
Espagnols à remettre en état le canon et à s'en servir.

PAGES 102/103
ON THE SET OF 'THE PRIDE AND THE
PASSION' (1957)
Director Kramer told Sinatra: "This may not be a great
film, but it will certainly be memorable." He wasn't
wrong. / Regisseur Kramer sagte zu Sinatra: „Das mag
vielleicht kein großer Film werden, aber man wird sich
sicherlich an ihn erinnern." / Kramer, le réalisateur, a
confié à Sinatra : « Ce n'est peut-être pas un grand film ;
mais c'est un film dont on se souviendra. »

ON THE SET OF 'THE PRIDE AND THE
PASSION' (1957)
Over the course of the film Cary Grant falls for Sophia
Loren's charms, which understandably causes friction
between him and Sinatra. / Im Laufe des Films erliegt
Anthony (Cary Grant) dem Charme von Juana (Sophia
Loren), was verständlicherweise zu Spannungen
zwischen ihm und Miguel führt. / Au cours du film,
Cary Grant tombe amoureux de Sophia Loren, ce qui
entraîne bien évidemment des frictions entre Sinatra
et lui.

STILL FROM 'THE JOKER IS WILD' (1957)
Sinatra plays Joe E. Lewis, a singer whose throat was slit
by gangsters. Sinatra knew what it was like for a singer
to lose his voice. / Sinatra spielt Joe E. Lewis, einen
Sänger, dem von Gangstern die Kehle aufgeschlitzt
wurde. Sinatra wusste ganz genau, wie es für einen
Sänger war, seine Stimme zu verlieren. / Sinatra joue
le rôle de Joe E. Lewis, un chanteur qui a eu la gorge
tranchée par des gangsters. Sinatra n'ignore pas ce que
c'est pour un chanteur que de perdre sa voix.

*"I feel sorry for people who don't drink. When they
wake up in the morning, that's as good as they're
going to feel all day."*
Frank Sinatra

*„Ich bedaure Menschen, die nicht trinken. Wenn
sie morgens aufwachen, dann ist das schon das
höchste aller Gefühle für den ganzen Tag."*
Frank Sinatra

STILL FROM 'THE JOKER IS WILD' (1957)
Lewis turned to gambling and alcohol, and made these
the subject of his comedy act. The song 'All the Way'
won an Oscar. / Lewis verfällt dem Glücksspiel und dem
Alkohol und macht sie zu den Themen seiner Auftritte
als Komiker. Das Lied „All the Way" wurde mit einem
„Oscar" ausgezeichnet. / Lewis se met à jouer et à
boire, et décide d'en faire une comédie. La chanson
« All the Way » obtiendra un oscar.

« Je plains les gens qui ne boivent pas. Quand ils se
réveillent le matin, ils savent qu'ils sont déjà au top
de leur forme ... pour toute la journée. »
Frank Sinatra

STILL FROM 'PAL JOEY' (1957)
Sinatra was reunited with his 'Anchors Aweigh' director
George Sidney for this adaptation of the 1940 Rodgers
and Hart musical. / Sinatra wurde in dieser Verfilmung
des Musicals von Rodgers and Hart aus dem Jahre 1940
wieder mit George Sidney vereint, dem Regisseur von
Urlaub in Hollywood. / Sinatra retrouva le réalisateur
d'*Escale à Hollywood*, George Sidney, pour cette
adaptation de la comédie musicale de Rodgers et Hart
(1940).

"A bum's a bum wherever he goes."
Joey Evans, 'Pal Joey' (1957)

„Ein Penner bleibt ein Penner, wo er auch hingeht."
Joey Evans, Pal Joey (1957)

« Un clodo sera toujours un clodo, où qu'il aille. »
Joey Evans, La Blonde ou la Rousse (1957)

STILL FROM 'PAL JOEY' (1957)
Playing a nightclub singer, Sinatra had the opportunity
to perform 'The Lady is a Tramp' and 'My Funny
Valentine.' / Die Rolle eines Nachtclubsängers gab
Sinatra Gelegenheit, „The Lady Is a Tramp" und
„My Funny Valentine" zu singen. / Sinatra tient le
rôle d'un chanteur de boîte de nuit, ce qui lui donne
l'occasion d'interpréter « The Lady is a Tramp » et « My
Funny Valentine ».

ON THE SET OF 'PAL JOEY' (1957)
In his element, Sinatra rehearses the dream number with co-stars Novak and Hayworth. / Ganz in seinem Element probt Sinatra hier die Traumnummer mit Novak und Hayworth. / Sinatra, dans son élément, répète la scène avec Novak et Hayworth.

PAGES 110/111
STILL FROM 'KINGS GO FORTH' (1958)
Sinatra is in a love triangle with Tony Curtis and half-caste Natalie Wood. Sinatra: "The message is that love can conquer anything, including racial and religious differences." / Loggins (Sinatra) ist Teil einer Dreiecksbeziehung mit Harris (Tony Curtis) und dem Halbblut Monique (Natalie Wood). / Sinatra dans un triangle amoureux avec Tony Curtis et l'actrice métissée Natalie Wood. Sinatra déclare : « Le message, c'est que l'amour peut venir à bout de toutes les difficultés. »

STILL FROM 'PAL JOEY' (1957)
Rita Hayworth and Kim Novak vie for Sinatra's attention in this dream number. / In dieser Traumsequenz wetteifern Vera (Rita Hayworth) und Linda (Kim Novak) um Joeys Aufmerksamkeit. / Rita Hayworth et Kim Novak rivalisent pour obtenir les faveurs de Sinatra dans cette scène de rêve.

STILL FROM 'SOME CAME RUNNING' (1958)
He co-starred for the first time with Rat Pack buddy
Dean Martin (right), with Shirley MacLaine as the naïve
Ginnie. / Zum ersten Mal stand er in diesem Film mit
Dean Martin (rechts), seinem Kumpel aus dem „Rat
Pack", vor der Kamera – neben Shirley MacLaine in der
Rolle der naiven Ginnie. / Il joue pour la première fois
avec Dean Martin (à droite), un copain de la célèbre
bande appelée le «Rat Pack», avec Shirley MacLaine
dans le rôle de la naïve Ginnie.

**PORTRAIT FOR 'SOME CAME RUNNING'
(1958)**
Back at MGM in a straight dramatic part, Sinatra, here
with Martha Hyer, portrayed the troubled soldier/writer
of James Jones' novel. / Wieder bei MGM spielte
Sinatra – hier mit Martha Hyer – in einer dramatischen
Rolle den innerlich aufgewühlten Soldaten und
Schriftsteller aus dem Roman von James Jones. /
De retour à la MGM dans un rôle dramatique, Sinatra,
ici avec Martha Hyer, incarne l'écrivain soldat perturbé
du roman de James Jones.

STILL FROM 'SOME CAME RUNNING' (1958)

STILL FROM 'SOME CAME RUNNING' (1958)
Sinatra gives one of his best performances as the
embittered, hard-drinking writer unable to reconcile his
art and his life. / Sinatra liefert hier eine seiner besten
Schauspielerleistungen als verbitterter, trunksüchtiger
Schriftsteller. / Sinatra en écrivain aigri et alcoolique
interprète là un des plus beaux rôles de sa carrière.

STILL FROM 'A HOLE IN THE HEAD' (1959)
With Edward G. Robinson as his older brother. Sinatra
recorded a special version of the Oscar-winning theme
song 'High Hopes' for John F. Kennedy's presidential
campaign. / Mit Edward G. Robinson in der Rolle
seines älteren Bruders. Sinatra nahm eine spezielle
Version des mit dem „Oscar" ausgezeichneten Lieds
„High Hopes" als musikalisches Thema für den
Präsidentschaftswahlkampf von John F. Kennedy auf. /
Ici avec Edward G. Robinson dans le rôle du frère aîné.
Sinatra enregistre pour la campagne présidentielle de
John F. Kennedy une version spéciale de « High Hopes »,
la chanson de la bande originale récompensée par un
oscar.

STILL FROM 'A HOLE IN THE HEAD' (1959)
Sinatra's first outright comedy in many years
portraying a bachelor Italian/American father for
director/producer Frank Capra. / In seiner ersten
reinen Komödie seit vielen Jahren spielte Sinatra unter
der Regie von Frank Capra einen italoamerikanischen
alleinerziehenden Vater. / Dirigé par Frank Capra, il joue
le rôle d'un père célibataire italo-américain. C'est la
seule vraie comédie qu'ait tournée Sinatra pendant
toutes ces années.

CARTOON FOR 'NEVER SO FEW' (1959)
A promotional cartoon depicts Sinatra and co-star Gina
Lollobrigida. / Eine Werbekarikatur zeigt Sinatra und
seine Kollegin Gina Lollobrigida. / Sinatra et l'actrice
Gina Lollobrigida dans un dessin humoristique destiné à
promouvoir le film.

POSTER FOR 'NEVER SO FEW' (1959)
This Italian poster depicts Richard Johnson, Sinatra,
Steve McQueen and Charles Bronson in action. /
Dieses italienische Filmplakat zeigt Richard Johnson,
Frank Sinatra, Steve McQueen und Charles Bronson in
Aktion. / Sur cette affiche italienne, on voit les acteurs
Richard Johnson, Sinatra, Steve McQueen et Charles
Bronson en action.

i 4 CHE NON VOLEVANO MORIRE

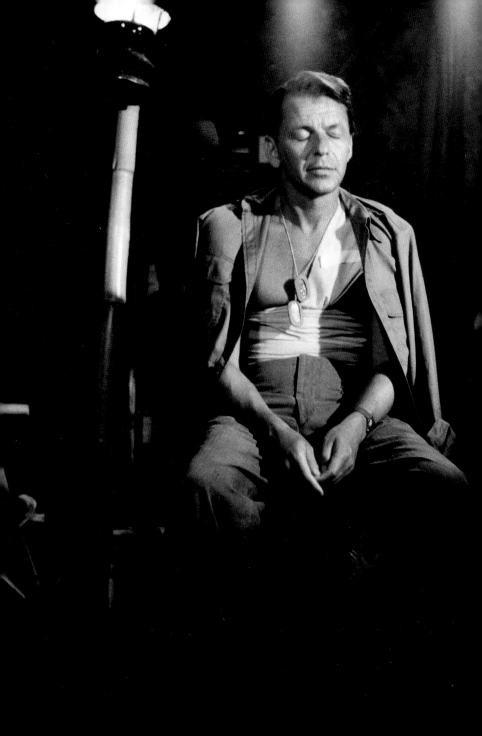

*"You know, the movies have got it all wrong —
a cigarette tastes lousy when you're wounded."*
Capt. Tom Reynolds, 'Never So Few' (1959)

„*Weißt du, die Filme lügen — wenn man verletzt ist,
dann schmeckt eine Zigarette lausig.*"
Captain Tom Reynolds, *Wenn das Blut kocht* (1959)

« *Tu sais, les films se trompent sur toute la ligne :
y a rien de pire qu'une clope quand t'es blessé.* »
Capitaine Tom Reynolds, *La Proie des vautours* (1959)

STILL FROM 'NEVER SO FEW' (1959)
In Burma to train the natives to fight, the situation
becomes increasingly desperate for Sinatra's men as
Japanese soldiers and Chinese rebels close in. /
Für die Männer um Captain Reynolds (Sinatra), die
Einheimische in Birma zum Kampf ausbilden sollen,
wird die Lage zunehmend brenzliger, als die japanischen
Truppen und die chinesischen Rebellen immer näher
rücken. / Sinatra et ses hommes sont en Birmanie pour
apprendre aux autochtones à se battre, mais la situation
devient quasiment désespérée à mesure que les soldats
japonais et les rebelles chinois se rapprochent.

STILL FROM 'CAN-CAN' (1960)
Sinatra is the lawyer/boyfriend of Shirley MacLaine,
who owns the café where the illegal can-can dance is
performed. Maurice Chevalier (center) is a helpful
judge. / Sinatra spielt den Anwalt und Freund von
Simone (Shirley MacLaine), der das Café gehört, indem
illegal Cancan-Tänze aufgeführt werden. Maurice
Chevalier (Mitte) mimt einen hilfsbereiten Richter. /
L'avocat joué par Sinatra est le petit ami de Shirley
MacLaine, patronne du café où se pratique le cancan,
malgré l'interdiction de la loi. Maurice Chevalier (au
centre) interprète un juge bienveillant.

POSTER FOR 'CAN-CAN' (1960)
Shirley MacLaine became a sort of mascot for the Rat
Pack. / Shirley MacLaine wurde für das „Rat Pack" zu
einer Art Maskottchen. / Shirley MacLaine devient en
quelque sorte la mascotte du Rat Pack.

ON THE SET OF 'OCEAN'S ELEVEN' (1960)
Although not an official producer, Sinatra was not above telling director Lewis Milestone (under camera) what to do. / Obwohl er den Film offiziell nicht produzierte, scheute sich Sinatra nicht, Regisseur Lewis Milestone (unterhalb der Kamera) zu sagen, was er zu tun habe. / Sinatra n'était pas officiellement le producteur du film, mais il n'hésitait pas à donner son avis au réalisateur Lewis Milestone (sous la caméra).

STILL FROM 'OCEAN'S ELEVEN' (1960)
The first of several Rat Pack movies with Dean Martin, Peter Lawford, Sinatra, Joey Bishop, and Sammy Davis Jr. (not pictured). / Der erste von mehreren „Rat Pack"-Spielfilmen mit Dean Martin, Peter Lawford, Frank Sinatra, Joey Bishop und Sammy Davis, Jr. (nicht im Bild). / Le premier film du Rat Pack avec Dean Martin, Peter Lawford, Sinatra, Joey Bishop et Sammy Davis Jr, qui ne figure pas sur la photo.

STILL FROM 'OCEAN'S ELEVEN' (1960)
Danny Ocean is romantically entangled with Patrice
Wymore. / Danny Ocean hat ein Verhältnis mit Adele
(Patrice Wymore). / Danny Ocean dans un imbroglio
romantique avec Patrice Wymore.

"The reason nobody's gone to the moon yet:
no equipment."
Danny Ocean, 'Ocean's Eleven' (1960)

„Der Grund, warum noch niemand zum Mond
geflogen ist: keine Ausrüstung."
Danny Ocean, *Frankie und seine Spießgesellen* (1960)

« Pourquoi personne n'est encore jamais allé sur
la lune ? Y a pas le matos. »
Danny Ocean, *L'Inconnu de Las Vegas* (1960)

STILL FROM 'OCEAN'S ELEVEN' (1960)
Above all this is a heist movie. Sinatra said, "Not a great movie like 'Gone With the Wind,' but something the public can enjoy. It's called entertainment." / In erster Linie geht es in diesem Film um einen Raubüberfall. Sinatra meinte: „Kein großer Film wie *Vom Winde verweht*, aber etwas, an dem das Publikum seinen Spaß hat. Man nennt das Unterhaltung." / Ce film raconte l'histoire d'un hold-up. Sinatra déclara: « Ce n'est pas un grand film comme *Autant en emporte le vent*, mais c'est un film de "divertissement", par conséquent il plaira au grand public. »

STILL FROM 'THE DEVIL AT 4 O'CLOCK' (1961)
Always respectful of veteran actors, Sinatra gave top
billing to Spencer Tracy, a fellow member of the original
Bogart Rat Pack. / Sinatra, der seine älteren Kollegen
stets respektierte, ließ Spencer Tracy, einem Kollegen
aus dem Original-„Rat Pack" um Bogart, den Vortritt in
der Titelnennung. / Toujours respectueux de ses aînés,
Sinatra laisse le haut de l'affiche à Spencer Tracy, un des
membres fondateurs du Rat Pack de Bogart.

**ON THE SET OF 'THE DEVIL AT 4 O'CLOCK'
(1961)**
As he entered middle age, Sinatra gravitated towards
projects that were less dramatic and had a relaxed
atmosphere. / Mit zunehmendem Alter fühlte sich
Sinatra eher zu Filmen hingezogen, die weniger dra-
matisch waren und in einer eher entspannten Atmo-
sphäre gedreht wurden. / Dans la seconde moitié de sa
vie, Sinatra s'oriente vers des films à l'atmosphère moins
dramatique et plus détendue.

PORTRAIT (CIRCA 1957)
At this stage in his career Sinatra was earning $4 million
a year. / In diesem Stadium seiner Karriere verdiente
Sinatra vier Millionen Dollar im Jahr. / À ce stade de sa
carrière, Sinatra gagne quatre millions de dollars par an.

PORTRAIT FOR 'SERGEANTS 3' (1962)
John Sturges directed the second Rat Pack movie, a
remake of 'Gunga Din' transposed to the West. Each
evening Sinatra's private jet took them to Las Vegas to
do a show. / John Sturges führte beim zweiten „Rat
Pack"-Film Regie, einem in den Wilden Westen
verlegten Remake von *Aufstand in Sidi Hakim*. Jeden
Abend flogen sie im Privatjet nach Las Vegas, um dort
auf der Bühne zu stehen. / John Sturges dirige le
second film du Rat Pack, un remake de *Gunga Din*
transposé dans le monde occidental. Tous les soirs
Sinatra emmène les acteurs se produire à Las Vegas
dans son jet privé.

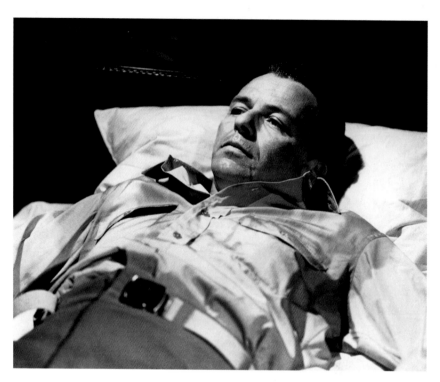

STILL FROM 'THE MANCHURIAN CANDIDATE' (1962)
The disturbed Major Marco is one of Sinatra's most powerful (and unrecognized) performances. He is the fulcrum of the John Frankenheimer/George Axelrod adaptation of Richard Condon's darkly comic political thriller. / Der geistig verwirrte Major Marco gehört zu Sinatras stärksten (und verkannten) Leistungen. Er ist der Dreh- und Angelpunkt der John Frankenheimer/George Axelrod-Verfilmung des düster-komischen Politthrillers von Richard Condon. / Le personnage trouble du major Marco est un des plus grands rôles de Sinatra et un des moins connus. Il est au centre de l'adaptation cinématographique par John Frankenheimer et George Axelrod du roman de Richard Condon, un thriller politique à l'humour noir.

STILL FROM 'THE MANCHURIAN CANDIDATE' (1962)
Sinatra plays an ex-Korean prisoner-of-war who realizes his commanding officer has been brainwashed into assassinating a Presidential nominee. / Sinatra spielt einen Soldaten, der aus koreanischer Kriegsgefangenschaft heimgekehrt ist und nun feststellen muss, dass sein Vorgesetzter nach einer Gehirnwäsche darauf angesetzt wurde, einen Präsidentschaftskandidaten zu ermorden. / Cet ancien prisonnier pendant la guerre de Corée s'aperçoit que son officier supérieur a subi un lavage de cerveau et s'apprête à assassiner un candidat à la présidence.

STILL FROM 'THE MANCHURIAN CANDIDATE' (1962)

Major Marco finds out that the "unloveable" Raymond Shaw (Laurence Harvey) is triggered by the Queen of Diamonds playing card. / Major Marco findet heraus, dass die Karo-Dame bei dem „nicht liebenswerten" Raymond Shaw (Laurence Harvey) den Impuls zum Töten auslöst. / Le major Marco découvre que l'inquiétant Raymond Shaw (Laurence Harvey) est sous influence et qu'il réagit à la reine de carreau.

STILL FROM 'THE MANCHURIAN CANDIDATE' (1962)

Although approaching fifty, Sinatra did not shy away from action sequences such as this martial arts encounter with Henry Silva. / Obwohl er schon auf die Fünfzig zusteuerte, scheute Sinatra nicht vor Actionszenen wie dieser zurück, in der er sich mit Henry Silva in asiatischer Kampfkunst misst. / À l'approche de la cinquantaine, Sinatra n'avait pas renoncé aux scènes d'action tel ce combat d'art martial avec Henry Silva.

**STILL FROM 'COME BLOW YOUR HORN'
(1963)**
A return to outright comedy and middle-aged romance
with co-star Barbara Rush. / Sinatra kehrte wieder zur
reinen Komödie und zu einer Romanze im reiferen Alter
zurück – hier mit Kollegin Barbara Rush. / Un retour à la
comédie pure et aux amours raisonnables avec Barbara
Rush.

**POSTER FOR 'COME BLOW YOUR HORN'
(1963)**
Filming the opening titles on location on Madison
Avenue, New York City, Sinatra walked out of a store,
sang, hailed a cab and was gone for the day. / Beim
Außendreh für die Titelsequenz an der Madison Avenue
in New York City kam Sinatra aus einem Geschäft, sang,
hielt ein Taxi an und war für den Rest des Tages
verschwunden. / Pour le tournage du générique, sur
Madison Avenue, à New York : Sinatra sort d'une
boutique, se met à chanter, hèle un taxi et disparaît.

STILL FROM 'FOUR FOR TEXAS' (1963)
Sinatra's relationship with director Robert Aldrich deteriorated to the extent that he was a bit nervous when Aldrich showed co-star Anita Ekberg how to draw the straight razor across his neck. / Sinatras Verhältnis zu Regisseur Robert Aldrich verschlechterte sich dermaßen, dass er ziemlich nervös wurde, als Aldrich Anita Ekberg zeigte, wie sie ihm das Rasiermesser an die Kehle legen sollte. / La relation entre Sinatra et le réalisateur Robert Aldrich s'est tellement dégradée que Sinatra se sent vaguement nerveux quand Aldrich montre à Anita Ekberg, sa partenaire dans le film, comment lui passer le rasoir sur la gorge.

STILL FROM 'FOUR FOR TEXAS' (1963)
Anita Ekberg and Ursula Andress did nude scenes, but they were censored, so only the action and comedy remains. / Anita Ekberg und Ursula Andress drehten Nacktszenen für den Film, die aber der Zensur zum Opfer fielen, sodass nur noch Action und Comedy übriggeblieben sind. / Les scènes de nu tournées par Anita Ekberg et Ursula Andress ayant été censurées, il ne reste que les scènes d'action et les scènes comiques.

STILL FROM 'ROBIN AND THE SEVEN HOODS' (1964)
Director Gene Kelly walked off the set because Sinatra would not rehearse. He was replaced by Gordon Douglas, who directed the last and weakest of the Rat Pack movies. / Regisseur Gene Kelly stieg aus dem Film aus, weil sich Sinatra weigerte, zu proben. Kelly wurde auf dem Regiestuhl dieses letzten und schwächsten „Rat Pack"-Films durch Gordon Douglas ersetzt. / Le réalisateur Gene Kelly part en claquant la porte parce que Sinatra refuse de répéter et c'est Gordon Douglas qui dirige le dernier et le moins bon des films du Rat Pack.

STILL FROM 'ROBIN AND THE SEVEN HOODS' (1964)
Bing Crosby becomes an honorary Rat Pack member. / Bing Crosby wird zum Ehrenmitglied des „Rat Packs" ernannt. / Bing Crosby devient membre honoraire du Rat Pack.

"You look like the day they fixed the electricity at the death house."
Robbo, 'Robin and the Seven Hoods' (1964)

„Du siehst aus wie an dem Tag, als man in der Todeszelle die Stromleitungen repariert hat."
Robbo, *Sieben gegen Chicago* (1964)

« À te voir, on se croirait dans le couloir de la mort le jour où ils ont rebranché le courant. »
Robbo, *Les Sept Voleurs de Chicago* (1964)

LA WARNER BROS. PRESENTA

LA TUA PELLE O LA MIA

STILL FROM 'NONE BUT THE BRAVE' (1965)
Sinatra's only attempt at feature film directing, a
sympathetic portrayal of ordinary soldiers on both sides
of a war. / Sinatras einziger Regieversuch bei einem
Spielfilm war ein einfühlsames Porträt gewöhnlicher
Soldaten auf beiden Seiten eines Krieges. / Le seul
film de Sinatra en tant que réalisateur : le portrait
empathique de soldats ordinaires des deux côtés du
front.

LEFT/LINKS/CI-CONTRE
POSTER FOR 'NONE BUT THE BRAVE' (1965)

PAGES 144 & 145
STILLS FROM 'VON RYAN'S EXPRESS' (1965)
In a riff on the highly successful 'Great Escape,' Sinatra's
character Colonel Von Ryan overcomes resistance from
fellow POWs and dies saving them. / Im Kielwasser
des außerordentlich erfolgreichen *Gesprengte Ketten*
überwindet der von Sinatra gespielte Colonel Ryan
den Widerstand seiner Mitkriegsgefangenen und stirbt
beim Versuch, sie zu retten. / Une variante du film à
succès *La Grande Évasion*, dans laquelle le personnage
du colonel Von Ryan, incarné par Sinatra, surmonte la
résistance de ses soldats, prisonniers de guerre
comme lui, et meurt en leur sauvant la vie.

STILL FROM 'MARRIAGE ON THE ROCKS'
(1965)
With Sinatra comfortable being fifty, the love interests
of his characters were no longer young women. / Sinatra
fühlte sich mit seinen 50 Jahren wohl, und seine Figuren
interessierten sich auch nicht mehr für junge Frauen. /
Sinatra assume bien ses cinquante ans, et les conquêtes
amoureuses des personnages qu'il interprète ne sont
plus de toutes jeunes femmes.

"He is the Mercedes-Benz of men."
Marlene Dietrich

„Er ist der Mercedes-Benz unter den Männern."
Marlene Dietrich

*« Si c'était une voiture, cet homme serait une
Mercedes. »*
Marlene Dietrich

**STILL FROM 'MARRIAGE ON THE ROCKS'
(1965)**
As an accidentally divorced ad man, Sinatra 'loses' wife
Deborah Kerr to Dean Martin and lets her dance with
Cesar Romero. / Als versehentlich geschiedener
Werbefachmann „verliert" Sinatra seine Frau (Deborah
Kerr) an seinen Freund Ernie (Dean Martin) und lässt sie
mit Miguel (Cesar Romero) tanzen. / Publicitaire
divorcé par accident, Sinatra « abandonne » sa femme
Deborah Kerr à Dean Martin et la laisse danser avec
Cesar Romero.

STILL FROM 'CAST A GIANT SHADOW' (1966)
Always a champion of minority causes, Sinatra plays a small role (with Kirk Douglas and Yul Brynner) in this war film about the emergence of the Israeli state. / Sinatra, der sich stets für Minderheiten einsetzte, spielt eine kleine Rolle (mit Kirk Douglas und Yul Brynner) in diesem Kriegsfilm über die Entstehung des Staates Israel. / Éternel défenseur des causes minoritaires, Sinatra joue un petit rôle (avec Kirk Douglas et Yul Brynner) dans ce film de guerre qui raconte la naissance de l'État d'Israël.

STILL FROM 'CAST A GIANT SHADOW' (1966)
True story: Vince Talmadge dropped soda siphons from his plane during the war — the whistling and loud crash distracted the enemy. / Eine wahre Geschichte: Vince Talmadge warf aus seinem Bomber Siphonflaschen heraus, um durch das Pfeifen und den lauten Knall beim Aufprall den Feind abzulenken. / Une anecdote authentique : pendant la guerre, Vince Talmadge a jeté des siphons d'eau de Seltz depuis son avion, parvenant ainsi, grâce au sifflement et au fracas de la cargaison, à détourner l'attention de l'ennemi.

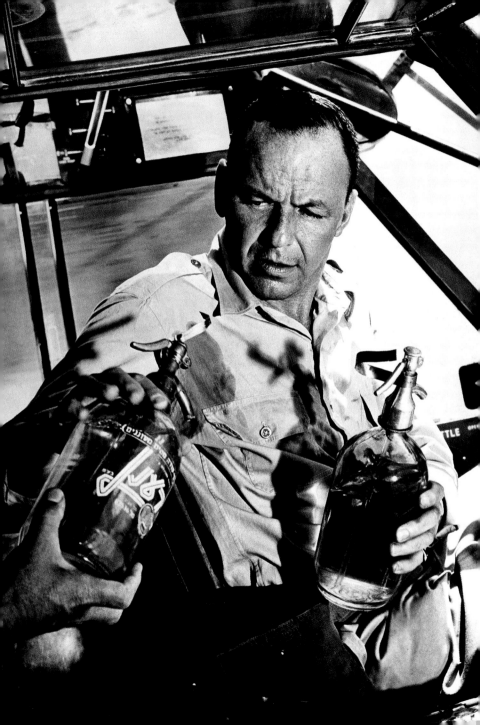

POSTER FOR 'ASSAULT ON A QUEEN' (1966)

STILL FROM 'ASSAULT ON A QUEEN' (1966)
Sinatra's expression inside the diving suit betrays his
lack of enthusiasm for this uninspired action film. /
Sinatras Gesichtsausdruck im Taucheranzug verrät,
dass er von diesem einfallslosen Actionfilm nicht
sonderlich begeistert war. / La moue de Sinatra dans
sa combinaison de plongée trahit son manque
d'enthousiasme pour ce film d'action sans intérêt.

STILL FROM 'THE NAKED RUNNER' (1967)
Sinatra plays a distinguished industrialist drawn into
the Cold War. / Sinatra spielt einen bedeutenden
Industriellen, der in den Kalten Krieg verstrickt wird. /
Sinatra joue le rôle d'un industriel, personnage distingué
impliqué dans la guerre froide.

RIGHT/RECHTS/CI-CONTRE
POSTER FOR 'THE NAKED RUNNER' (1967)

PAGES 154/155
POSTER FOR 'THE NAKED RUNNER' (1967)

FRANK SINATRA
ATRAPADO

PETER VAUGHAN • DERREN NESBITT • NADIA GRAY • TOBY ROBINS • INGER STRATTON • BASADA EN LA NOVELA DE FRANCIS CLIFFORD • GUION STANLEY MANN

PRODUCTOR BRAD DEXTER • DIRECTOR SIDNEY J. FURIE • SINATRA ENTERPRISES PRODUCTION • **TECHNICOLOR TECHNISCOPE**

K SINATRA
SU COLPO

PETER VAUGHAN · DERREN NESBITT
NADIA GRAY · TOBY ROBINS · INGER STRATTON
TRATTO DAL RACCONTO DI FRANCIS CLIFFORD

FRANK
SINATRA
E'

ON THE SET OF 'TONY ROME' (1967)
Sinatra plays ex-cop and private eye Tony Rome with co-star Jill St. John. / Sinatra spielt den ehemaligen Polizisten und jetzigen Privatdetektiv Tony Rome an der Seite von Jill St. John. / Sinatra incarne Tony Rome, ex-flic et détective privé. Il a pour partenaire Jill St. John.

POSTER FOR 'TONY ROME' (1967)

STILL FROM 'TONY ROME' (1967)
A millionaire developer is attacked as Tony Rome tries
to track down some stolen jewelry. / Während Tony
Rome nach gestohlenem Schmuck sucht, wird ein
Baulöwe angegriffen. / Un promoteur millionnaire est
attaqué alors que Tony Rome essaie de retrouver la
trace de bijoux volés.

STILL FROM 'TONY ROME' (1967)
Sinatra returned to the form of years past fighting
heavies in a last hurrah of action scenes. / Sinatra fand
zur Form früherer Jahre zurück, als er in seinen letzten
Actionszenen wieder schwere Jungs verprügelte. /
Sinatra revient aux films de ses débuts et tourne une
dernière série de scènes d'action, comme cette bagarre
avec de gros costauds.

STILL FROM 'TONY ROME' (1967)
He isn't afraid to investigate both high and low society, and is accepting of all races, creeds, and sexualities. / Er scheut sich nicht, in allen Gesellschaftsschichten zu ermitteln, und er akzeptiert alle Rassen, Religionen und sexuellen Präferenzen. / Il n'hésite pas à enquêter dans toutes les classes sociales, faisant preuve de tolérance envers chacun, quelle que soit sa race, sa religion ou sa sexualité.

STILL FROM 'TONY ROME' (1967)
Tony Rome gently inspects a girl who was beaten up because she talked to him – Tony makes the guy pay! / Tony Rome schaut sich zärtlich ein Mädchen an, das verprügelt wurde, weil es mit Tony gesprochen hatte. Er wird es dem Täter heimzahlen! / Tony Rome examine une jeune fille qui a reçu une raclée pour lui avoir adressé la parole – puis il fait payer le coupable!

"Frank once told me that the only way to negotiate a dispute was to kick the disputant in the ankles and, as he hopped around on one foot, belt him soundly in the chops."
Richard Condon, author

„Frank hat mir einmal erzählt, die einzige Art, einen Streit zu schlichten, sei, dem Gegner gegen's Schienbein zu treten, und ihm dann, wenn er auf einem Bein rumhüpft, einen kräftigen Kinnhaken zu verpassen."
Richard Condon, Schriftsteller

« Frank m'a déclaré un jour que la seule manière de régler un conflit, c'est d'envoyer un coup de pied dans la cheville de l'adversaire, et de profiter de ce que le type sautille sur l'autre pied pour lui démolir le portrait. »
Richard Condon, auteur

STILL FROM 'THE DETECTIVE' (1968)
Sinatra's police detective is troubled because he manipulates a confession out of this mentally unstable suspect to gain a promotion. / Der von Sinatra gespielte Kripobeamte ist in Schwierigkeiten, weil er diesen geistig verwirrten Verdächtigen zu einem Geständnis zwang, um befördert zu werden. / Le détective incarné par Sinatra est mal à l'aise parce qu'il a extorqué un aveu à un suspect qui n'a pas toute sa tête pour obtenir une promotion.

PAGES 164/165
STILL FROM 'THE DETECTIVE' (1968)
This superior police procedural abhors clichés. Sinatra has trouble with his wife (Lee Remick) because she is compelled to sleep with other men. / Dieser überragende Polizeifilm geht allen Klischees aus dem Weg. Leland (Sinatra) hat Probleme mit seiner Frau (Lee Remick), weil sie zwanghaft mit anderen Männern schläft. / Cet excellent film policier rejette tous les clichés du genre. Sinatra a des problèmes avec sa femme (Lee Remick) parce qu'elle est obligée de coucher avec d'autres hommes.

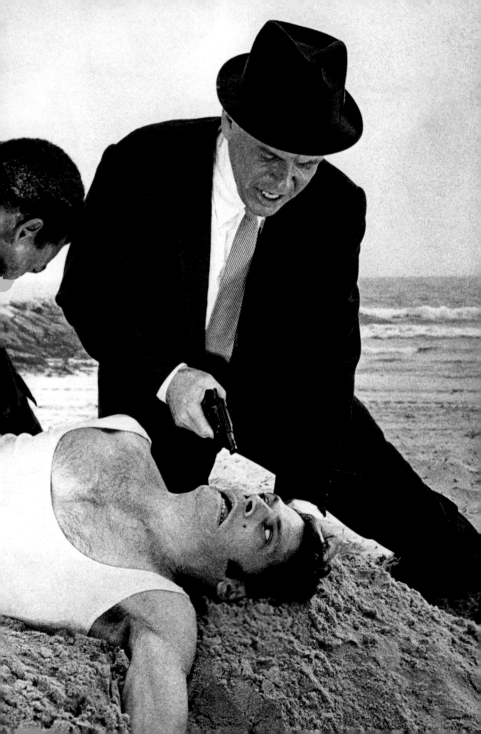

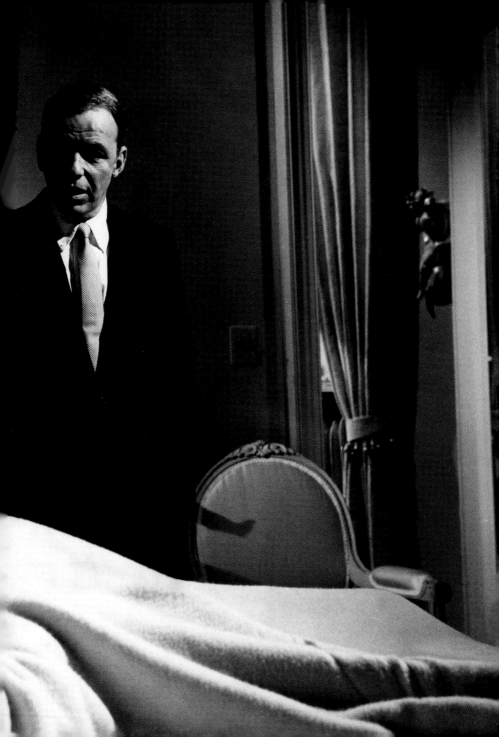

ON THE SET OF 'THE DETECTIVE' (1968)
Although there was a lot of location filming in New York
City, director Gordon Douglas (right) shot much of it on
a Hollywood backlot. / Obwohl zahlreiche Szenen vor
Ort in New York City entstanden, drehte Regisseur
Gordon Douglas (rechts) auch viele auf einem Studio-
gelände in Hollywood. / Si beaucoup de scènes ont été
tournées à New York, le réalisateur Gordon Douglas en
a également filmé une bonne partie dans un terrain
vague de Hollywood.

"I think each person knows what's important to him and he should compromise for nobody."
Det. Sgt. Joe Leland, 'The Detective' (1968)

„Ich denke, jeder weiß, was einem wichtig ist, und man sollte für niemanden Kompromisse eingehen."
Detective Sergeant Joe Leland, *Der Detektiv* (1968)

« On croit tous en quelque chose et on ne devrait jamais faire de concessions. Pour personne. »
Détective Joe Leland, *Le Détective* (1968)

ON THE SET OF 'LADY IN CEMENT' (1968)
Raquel Welch is Sinatra's romantic interest in this
lackluster film, which features many Sinatra in-jokes for
the hardcore fans. / Raquel Welch spielt Tony Romes
Geliebte in diesem glanzlosen Film, der viele
Anspielungen für hartgesottene Sinatra-Fans enthält. /
Dans ce film sans intérêt, Sinatra est amoureux de
Raquel Welch. Le script est par ailleurs truffé de clins
d'œil cocasses destinés aux inconditionnels de Sinatra.

STILL FROM 'LADY IN CEMENT' (1968)
In the opening sequence, treasure-diving Tony Rome
discovers the lady of the title being menaced by a
shark. / In der Eröffnungssequenz entdeckt
Schatztaucher Tony Rome, wie die Lady aus dem Titel
von einem Hai bedroht wird. / Dans les premières
images du film, Tony Rome, plongeur et chasseur de
trésors, rencontre l'héroïne alors qu'elle est menacée
par un requin.

"Frank is the only person I know who invites you
to a black-tie party and, as he hangs up, says,
'Be sure and bring your sunglasses.'"
Harry Kurnitz, screenwriter

„Frank ist der einzige Mensch, den ich kenne, der
dich zu einer Party mit Abendgarderobe einlädt
und vor dem Auflegen noch sagt: ‚Und vergiss
deine Sonnenbrille nicht!'."
Harry Kurnitz, Drehbuchautor

« Frank est capable de vous inviter à une soirée
où le smoking est de rigueur et d'ajouter avant de
raccrocher : "Et surtout n'oublie pas tes lunettes de
soleil." »
Harry Kurnitz, scénariste

**ON THE SET OF 'DIRTY DINGUS MAGEE'
(1970)**
Sinatra's sense of humor was beginning to wear thin, like
his long johns. / Der Film stellte Sinatras Sinn für Humor
auf eine harte Probe — und seine langen Unterhosen
ebenfalls. / Le sens de l'humour de Sinatra commençait
à s'user, tout comme son caleçon.

STILL FROM 'DIRTY DINGUS MAGEE' (1970)
Dirty Dingus Magee is a good-for-nothing, lowdown
thief and swindler looking for money and gold. / Dirty
Dingus Magee ist ein gemeiner Dieb, Schwindler und
Taugenichts, der Geld und Gold sucht. / Dirty Dingus
Magee est un bon à rien, un voleur méprisable et un
arnaqueur en quête d'argent et de métal fin.

"Frank takes things seriously. I don't."
Dean Martin, singer/actor

„Frank nimmt die Dinge ernst. Ich nicht."
Dean Martin, Sänger/Schauspieler

« Frank prend les choses au sérieux. Moi pas. »
Dean Martin, chanteur/acteur

STILL FROM 'DIRTY DINGUS MAGEE' (1970)
A Rat Pack movie without the Rat Pack which relies too heavily on overwrought pratfalls. / Ein „Rat Pack"-Film ohne das „Rat Pack", der sich zu sehr auf übertriebenen Slapstick stützt. / Un film du Rat Pack sans les membres du groupe ; l'intrigue repose sur une série de rebondissements tirés par les cheveux.

PAGES 174/175
STILL FROM 'THE FIRST DEADLY SIN' (1980)
Luger in hand and nearing retirement, Sinatra's policeman is on the trail of a serial killer. / Mit der Luger in der Hand und kurz vor dem Ruhestand verfolgt Sinatra als Polizist einen Serienkiller. / Armé d'un pistolet Luger, le policier campé par Sinatra, qui approche de la retraite, est sur la piste d'un tueur en série.

ON THE SET OF 'CANNONBALL RUN II' (1984)
Sinatra poses with the last of the Rat Packers: Dean
Martin, Sammy Davis, Jr., and Shirley MacLaine. / Sinatra
posiert mit dem Rest des „Rat Packs": Dean Martin,
Sammy Davis, Jr., und Shirley MacLaine. / Sinatra pose
avec les seuls membres du Rat Pack encore en vie :
Dean Martin, Sammy Davis Jr et Shirley MacLaine.

"Rock and Roll people love Frank Sinatra because
Frank has got what we want: swagger and
attitude. He's big on attitude, serious attitude,
bad attitude. Frank's the chairman of the bad."
Bono, singer/songwriter

„Rock-and-Roll-Menschen lieben Frank Sinatra,
weil Frank das hat, was wir uns wünschen:
prahlerisches Auftreten und Haltung. In Haltung
ist er groß: ernste Haltung, ablehnende Haltung.
Frank ist der Meister der Ablehnung."
Bono, Sänger/Songwriter

PORTRAIT
Although movies were behind him, Sinatra never retired from singing and continued to perform until just before his death. / Obwohl er keine Filme mehr drehte, hörte Sinatra nie auf zu singen und stand noch bis kurz vor seinem Tod auf der Bühne. / Longtemps après avoir cessé de faire du cinéma, Sinatra chantait encore ; il continuera de se produire jusqu'à sa mort.

PAGE 178
COVER OF 'MOVIE STORY' (AUGUST 1944)

« Nous les rockers, on adore Frank Sinatra parce qu'il a tout ce qui compte à nos yeux : l'arrogance et la frime. Il est très fort sur la frime, il sait la jouer sérieux ou salaud. Frank, c'est le roi des mauvais garçons. »
Bono, auteur et interprète du groupe U2

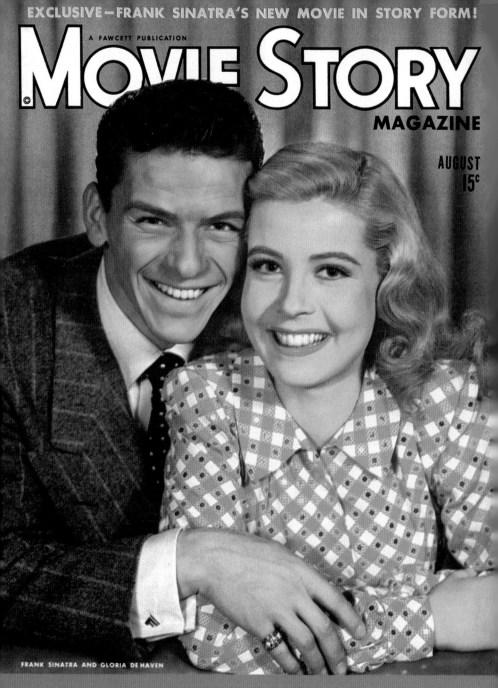

EXCLUSIVE—FRANK SINATRA'S NEW MOVIE IN STORY FORM!

A FAWCETT PUBLICATION

MOVIE STORY MAGAZINE

AUGUST
15c

FRANK SINATRA AND GLORIA DE HAVEN

NEW PICTURES WITH GARY COOPER, INGRID BERGMAN, FRED MacMURRAY
BARBARA STANWYCK, EDDIE BRACKEN, ELLA RAINES, RED SKELTON

3
CHRONOLOGY

CHRONOLOGIE

CHRONOLOGIE

CHRONOLOGY

12 December 1915 Born in Hoboken, New Jersey to Natalie Catherine 'Dolly' Garavente and Martin Sinatra.

1939 Signs two-year contract with Harry James Orchestra and issues first recordings. Marries Nancy Barbato.

1940 Joins Tommy Dorsey Band.

1941 First feature film appearance in *Las Vegas Nights*. Named Outstanding Male Vocalist by *Billboard*.

1942 Tries to enlist in the armed forces but is refused because of a punctured eardrum. First solo recording for RCA.

1945 Signs film contract with MGM.

1946 Named Favorite Male Singer *(Downbeat)* and Most Popular Screen Star *(Modern Screen)*. Receives special Academy Award for anti-racist short *The House I Live In*. Sings at "Lucky" Luciano's Christmas party.

1950 *The Frank Sinatra Show* lasts one season on TV.

1951 Divorces Barbato and marries Ava Gardner.

1952 Unable to sing because of damaged vocal cords, dropped by Columbia Records and MCA agency. Campaigns for part of Maggio in *From Here to Eternity*.

1953 Signs with Capitol Records.

1954 Receives Academy Award for Best Supporting Actor in *From Here to Eternity*. Divorces Gardner.

1955 Appears on television in *Our Town* and receives Emmy Award for song 'Love and Marriage.' August: on cover of *Time*.

1956 Best Actor nomination for *The Man with the Golden Arm*.

1957 *The Frank Sinatra Show* returns for one more season. With Humphrey Bogart's death, becomes de facto head of the Rat Pack and considers marriage with Bogart's widow, Lauren Bacall.

1959 Grammy Awards for Album of the Year and Male Vocalist.

1960 Grammy for Best Soundtrack, *Can-Can*. Campaigns energetically for John F. Kennedy, who makes a special version of 'High Hopes' his theme song.

1961 Moves to Reprise label. Produces Kennedy inaugural ball.

1963 In December, son Frank Jr. is kidnapped, held hostage for a week, and released after payment of a $250,000 ransom.

1965 Receives Emmy and Peabody Awards for *Sinatra: A Man and his Music*. Grammy Awards again for Album of the Year and Male Vocalist.

1966 Marries Mia Farrow. Third Grammy Awards for Album of the Year and Male Vocalist.

1968 Divorces Farrow.

1971 Receives Jean Hersholt Humanitarian Award.

1973 Returns from retirement with a new album and television special.

1976 Marries Barbara Marx.

1985 President Ronald Reagan, whose inaugural event Sinatra produces, awards him a Medal of Freedom.

1987 Lifetime achievement award from the National Association for the Advancement of Colored People.

1988 World concert tour with Dean Martin and Sammy Davis Jr.

1994 Receives the Grammy Legend award.

1995 Final performance in Palm Springs, California.

14 May 1998 Dies in Los Angeles.

ON THE SET OF 'THE KISSING BANDIT' (1948)

CHRONOLOGIE

12. Dezember 1915 Er kommt in Hoboken (New Jersey) zur Welt.

1939 Er schließt einen Zweijahresvertrag mit dem Harry James Orchestra und veröffentlicht seine ersten Aufnahmen. Er heiratet Nancy Barbato.

1940 Er schließt sich der Tommy-Dorsey-Band an.

1941 In *Las Vegas Nights* tritt er erstmals in einem Spielfilm auf. Die Zeitschrift *Billboard* kürt ihn zum „herausragenden männlichen Sänger".

1942 Er meldet sich zum Militärdienst, wird aber für untauglich befunden. Er macht seine erste Soloaufnahme für RCA.

1945 Er schließt einen Filmvertrag mit MGM ab.

1946 Er wird zum männlichen Lieblingssänger *(Downbeat)* und zum beliebtesten Filmstar *(Modern Screen)* gewählt. Er erhält einen speziellen Academy Award für den Kurzfilm *The House I Live In*. Er singt auf der Weihnachtsfeier des Mafiosos „Lucky" Luciano.

1950 *The Frank Sinatra Show* im Fernsehen wird nach nur einer Saison abgesetzt.

1951 Scheidung von Barbato, Heirat mit Ava Gardner.

1952 Er erleidet eine Verletzung der Stimmbänder. Columbia Records und die Agentur MCA lassen ihn fallen. Er bemüht sich um die Rolle des Gefreiten Maggio in *Verdammt in alle Ewigkeit*.

1953 Er schließt einen Vertrag mit Capitol Records.

1954 Er erhält einen Academy Award („Oscar") als bester Darsteller in einer Nebenrolle für *Verdammt in alle Ewigkeit*. Er lässt sich von Gardner scheiden.

1955 Er tritt im Fernsehen in *Unsere kleine Stadt* auf. Er erhält einen Emmy Award für „Love and Marriage". Im August erscheint er auf dem Titelbild von *Time*.

1956 Er wird für einen „Oscar" als bester Hauptdarsteller in *Der Mann mit dem goldenen Arm* nominiert.

PORTRAIT (1954)
Sinatra is proud to have won an Oscar for his portrayal of Pvt. Angelo Maggio in 'From Here to Eternity.' / Sinatra ist stolz darauf, dass seine Darstellung des Gefreiten Angelo Maggio in *Verdammt in alle Ewigkeit* mit einem „Oscar" gewürdigt wurde. / Sinatra est fier d'avoir reçu un oscar pour son interprétation du soldat Angelo Maggio dans *Tant qu'il y aura des hommes*.

1957 *The Frank Sinatra Show* kehrt für eine weitere Saison ins Fernsehen zurück. Mit dem Tod von Humphrey Bogart wird er zum Anführer des „Rat Pack".

1959 Er erhält Grammys für das „Album des Jahres" und als männlicher Sänger.

1960 Er erhält einen Grammy für den besten Soundtrack für *Ganz Paris träumt von der Liebe*. Er setzt sich im Wahlkampf vehement für John F. Kennedy ein.

1961 Er wechselt zur Plattenfirma Reprise. Er produziert den Ball zur Amtseinführung von Kennedy.

1963 Im Dezember wird sein Sohn Frank, Jr., entführt, eine Woche lang als Geisel gehalten und schließlich gegen eine Zahlung von $250.000 Lösegeld wieder freigelassen.

1965 Er erhält einen Emmy und einen Peabody Award für *Sinatra: A Man and his Music* sowie weitere Grammys („Album des Jahres" und „Männlicher Sänger").

1966 Er heiratet Mia Farrow. Er erhält seinen jeweils dritten Grammy Award für das „Album des Jahres" und als männlicher Sänger.

1968 Er lässt sich von Farrow scheiden.

1971 Er erhält den Jean Hersholt Humanitarian Award für sein soziales Engagement.

1973 Er kehrt mit einem neuen Album und einem Fernsehspecial aus dem Ruhestand zurück.

1976 Er heiratet Barbara Marx.

1985 Präsident Ronald Reagan verleiht ihm die Freiheitsmedaille.

1987 Er erhält einen Preis von der National Association for the Advancement of Colored People.

1988 Konzerttournee um die Welt mit Dean Martin und Sammy Davis, Jr.

1994 Er erhält den Grammy Legend Award für sein Lebenswerk.

1995 Letzter Auftritt in Palm Springs (Kalifornien).

14. Mai 1998 Er stirbt in Los Angeles.

CHRONOLOGIE

12 décembre 1915 Frank Sinatra voit le jour à Hoboken, New Jersey. Il est le fils de Natalie Catherine « Dolly » Garavente et Martin Sinatra.

1939 Signe un contrat de deux ans avec l'orchestre de Harry James et réalise ses premiers enregistrements. Épouse Nancy Barbato.

1940 Intègre l'orchestre de Tommy Dorsey.

1941 Première apparition au cinéma dans *Les Nuits de Las Vegas*. Élu meilleur chanteur de variétés par le magazine *Billboard*.

1942 Tente de s'engager, mais est réformé en raison d'un tympan perforé. Premier enregistrement en solo avec la maison de disques RCA.

1945 Signe un contrat avec la Metro Goldwin Mayer.

1946 *Downbeat* l'élit chanteur de l'année et *Modern Screen* acteur de cinéma le plus populaire. Il reçoit le prix spécial du jury aux Oscars pour un court métrage dénonçant le racisme, *The House I live in* et chante à la réception de Noël de « Lucky » Luciano.

1950 Son show télévisé, *The Frank Sinatra Show*, s'arrête dès l'issue de la première saison.

1951 Divorce de Nancy et épouse Ava Gardner.

1952 Un problème de cordes vocales l'empêche de chanter : Columbia Records et l'agence MCA le laissent tomber. Il se bat pour obtenir le rôle de Maggio dans *Tant qu'il y aura des hommes*.

1953 Signe avec la maison de disques Capitol Records.

1954 Reçoit l'oscar du Meilleur second rôle dans *Tant qu'il y aura des hommes*. Divorce d'Ava.

1955 Joue dans l'adaptation télévisée d'*Une Petite ville sans histoire* et reçoit un Emmy Award pour sa chanson « Love and Marriage ». En août de la même année, il fait la couverture du magazine *Time*.

1956 Nominé aux Oscars pour son interprétation dans *L'Homme au bras d'or*.

1957 Le *Frank Sinatra Show* revient au petit écran. Humphrey Bogart décède et Frank prend *de facto* la tête du Rat Pack. Il envisage d'épouser la veuve de Bogart, Lauren Bacall.

1959 Deux fois récompensé aux Grammy Awards : Album de l'année, Meilleur chanteur.

1960 Nouvelle récompense aux Grammy Awards pour la musique du film *Can-Can*. Soutient activement la candidature de John F. Kennedy : une version spéciale de « High Hopes » sert d'hymne à la campagne.

1961 Signe un contrat avec la maison de disques Reprise. Organise le gala inaugural de Kennedy.

1963 En décembre, son fils Frank Jr est kidnappé. Il sera libéré au bout d'une semaine, après versement d'une rançon de 250 000 dollars.

1965 Obtient un Emmy Award et un Peabody Award pour son album *A Man and his Music*. De nouveau récompensé aux Grammy Awards : Album de l'année, Meilleur chanteur.

1966 Épouse Mia Farrow. Troisième récompense aux GrammyAwards : Album de l'année, Meilleur chanteur.

1968 Divorce de Mia.

1971 Reçoit le prix humanitaire Jean Hersholt.

1973 Bien qu'en retraite, revient avec un nouvel album et un show télévisé exceptionnel.

1976 Épouse Barbara Marx.

1985 Organise le gala inaugural de Reagan ; cette année-là, le président lui décerne la médaille de la Liberté.

1987 Récompensé pour l'ensemble de son œuvre par l'association pour la défense des personnes de couleur.

1988 Tournée mondiale avec Dean Martin et Sammy Davis Jr.

1994 Reçoit la plus haute récompense aux Grammy Awards : figure légendaire de la musique.

1995 Dernier concert à Palm Springs, Californie.

14 mai 1998 Décède à Los Angeles.

PORTRAIT

FRANK SINATRA · ELEANOR PARKER · KIM NOVAK

THE
MAN
WITH
THE
GOLDEN
ARM

A FILM BY OTTO PREMINGER

With Arnold Stang, Darren McGavin, Robert Strauss, John Conte, Doro Merande, George E. Stone, George Mathews, Leonid Kinskey, Emile Meyer, Shorty Rogers, Shelly Manne,
Screenplay by Walter Newman & Lewis Meltzer. From the novel by Nelson Algren. Music by Elmer Bernstein. Produced & Directed by Otto Preminger. Released by United Artists

4
FILMOGRAPHY

FILMOGRAFIE

FILMOGRAPHIE

Lucky songstress Kathryn Grayson — with two such guys as Sinatra and Kelly after her heart!

Step Lively (1944)
Glen Russell. Director/Regie/réalisation: Tim Whelan.

Anchors Aweigh (dt. *Urlaub in Hollywood*, fr. *Escale à Hollywood*, 1945)
Clarence Doolittle. Director/Regie/réalisation: George Sidney.

It Happened in Brooklyn (dt. *Ihre beiden Verehrer*, fr. *Tout le monde chante*, 1947)
Danny Miller. Director/Regie/réalisation: Richard Whorf.

The Miracle of the Bells (dt. *Die Glocken von Coaltown*, fr. *Le Miracle des cloches*, 1948)
Father Paul/Pater Paul/Père Paul. Director/Regie/réalisation: Irving Pichel.

The Kissing Bandit (dt. *Ein Bandit zum Küssen*, fr. *Le Brigand amoureux*, 1949)
Ricardo. Director/Regie/réalisation: László Benedek.

Take Me Out to the Ball Game (dt. *Spiel zu dritt*, fr. *Match d'amour*, 1960)
Dennis Ryan. Director/Regie/réalisation: Busby Berkeley.

On the Town (dt. *Heut' gehn wir bummeln — Das ist New York*, fr. *Un jour à New York*, 1949)
Chip. Directors: Stanley Donen, Gene Kelly.

Double Dynamite (dt. *Doppeltes Dynamit*, 1951)
Johnny Dalton. Director/Regie/réalisation: Irving Cummings.

Meet Danny Wilson (dt. *Zu allem entschlossen*, fr. *Quand tu me souris*, 1952)
Danny Wilson. Director/Regie/réalisation: Joseph Chip. Directors: Staney Donen, Gene Kelly.

From Here to Eternity (dt. *Verdammt in alle Ewigkeit*, fr. *Tant qu'il y aura des hommes*, 1953)
Pvt. Angelo Maggio/Gefreiter Angelo Maggio/soldat Angelo Maggio. Director/Regie/réalisation: Fred Zinnemann.

Suddenly (dt. *Der Attentäter*, fr. *Je dois tuer*, 1954)
John Baron. Director/Regie/réalisation: Lewis Allen.

Young at Heart (dt. *Man soll nicht mit der Liebe spielen*, 1954)
Barney Sloan. Director/Regie/réalisation: Gordon Douglas.

Not as a Stranger (dt. ... und nicht als ein Fremder, fr. *Pour que vivent les hommes*, 1955)
Alfred Boone. Director/Regie/réalisation: Stanley Kramer.

Guys and Dolls (dt. *Schwere Jungen, leichte Mädchen*, fr. *Blanches colombes et vilains messieurs*, 1955)
Nathan Detroit. Director/Regie/réalisation: Joseph L. Mankewicz.

The Tender Trap (dt. *Die zarte Falle*, fr. *Le Tendre Piège*, 1955)
Charlie Y. Reader. Director/Regie/réalisation: Charles Walters.

The Man with the Golden Arm (dt. *Der Mann mit dem goldenen Arm*, fr. *L'Homme au bras d'or*, 1955)
Frankie Machine. Director/Regie/réalisation: Otto Preminger.

High Society (dt. *Die oberen Zehntausend*, fr. *La Haute Société*, 1956)
Mike Connor. Director/Regie/réalisation: Charles Walters.

Johnny Concho (dt. *Johnny Concho, der Bruder des Banditen*, 1956)
Johnny [also Producer/auch Produzent/également producteur]. Director/Regie/réalisation: Don McGuire.

Around the World in Eighty Days (dt. *In 80 Tagen um die Welt*, fr. *Le Tour du monde en 80 jours*, 1956)
Saloon pianist/pianiste de saloon. Director/Regie/réalisation: Michael Andersen.

The Pride and the Passion (dt. *Stolz und Leidenschaft*, fr. *Orgueil et passion*, 1957)
Miguel. Director/Regie/réalisation: Stanley Kramer.

The Joker Is Wild (dt. *Schicksalsmelodie*, fr. *Le Pantin brisé*, 1957)
Joe E. Lewis. Director/Regie/réalisation: C. Vidor.

Pal Joey (fr. *La Blonde ou la Rousse*, 1957)
Joey Evans. Director/Regie/réalisation: George Sidney.

Kings Go Forth (dt. *Rivalen*, fr. *Les Diables au soleil*, 1958)
1st Lt. Sam Loggins/1st Lieutenant Sam Loggins/Lieutenant Sam Loggins. Director/Regie/réalisation: Delmer Daves.

Some Came Running (dt. *Verdammt sind sie alle*, fr. *Comme un torrent*, 1958)
Dave Hirsh. Director/Regie/réalisation: Vincente Minnelli.

THE HILARIOUS LOW-DOWN ON HIGH LIFE!

THEY'RE ALL TOGETHER FOR THE FIRST TIME!

M-G-M PRESENTS IN VISTAVISION AND COLOR
A SOL C. SIEGEL PRODUCTION

**BING CROSBY
GRACE KELLY
FRANK SINATRA**
High Society
CELESTE HOLM · JOHN LUND
LOUIS CALHERN · SIDNEY BLACKMER
AND LOUIS ARMSTRONG AND HIS BAND
JOHN PATRICK · COLE PORTER
JOHNNY GREEN AND SAUL CHAPLIN · TECHNICOLOR · CHARLES WALTERS

A Hole in the Head (dt. *Eine Nummer zu groß*, fr. *Un trou dans la tête*, 1959)
Tony Manetta. Director/Regie/réalisation: Frank Capra.

Never So Few (dt. *Wenn das Blut kocht*, fr. *La Proie des vautours*, 1959)
Captain Tom Reynolds. Director/Regie/réalisation: John Sturges.

Can-Can (dt. *Ganz Paris träumt von der Liebe*, 1960)
François Durnais. Director/Regie/réalisation: Walter Lang.

Ocean's Eleven (dt. *Frankie und seine Spießgesellen*, fr. *L'Inconnu de Las Vegas*, 1960)
Danny Ocean. Director/Regie/réalisation: Lewis Milestone.

The Devil at 4 O'Clock (dt. *Der Teufel kommt um vier*, fr. *Le Diable à 4 heures*, 1961)
Harry. Director/Regie/réalisation: Mervyn LeRoy.

Sergeants 3 (dt. *Die siegreichen Drei*, fr. *Les Trois Sergents*, 1962)
Sergeant Mike Merry [also Producer/auch Produzent/également producteur].
Director/Regie/réalisation: John Sturges.

The Manchurian Candidate (dt. *Botschafter der Angst*, fr. *Un crime dans la tête*, 1962)
Major Bennett Marco. Director/Regie/réalisation: John Frankenheimer.

The List of Adrian Messenger (dt. *Die Totenliste*, fr. *Le Dernier de la liste*, 1963)
The Gypsy/Zigeuner/Le tzigane.
Director/Regie/réalisation: John Huston.

Come Blow Your Horn (dt. *Wenn mein Schlafzimmer sprechen könnte*, fr. *T'es plus dans la course, papa*, 1963)
Alan Baker. Director/Regie/réalisation: Bud Yorkin.

Four for Texas (dt. *Vier für Texas*, fr. *Quatre du Texas*, 1963)
Zack Thomas. Director/Regie/réalisation: Robert Aldrich.

Robin and the Seven Hoods (dt. *Sieben gegen Chicago*, fr. *Les Sept Voleurs de Chicago*, 1964)
Robbo [also Producer/auch Produzent/également producteur]. Director/Regie/réalisation: Gordon Douglas.

None But the Brave (dt. *Der Lohn der Mutigen*, fr. *L'Île des braves*, 1965)
Mate Maloney. Director & Producer/Regie und Produktion/réalisation et production: Frank Sinatra.

Von Ryan's Express (dt. *Colonel von Ryans Expreß*, fr. *L'Express du colonel Von Ryan*, 1965)
Colonel Joseph Ryan. Director/Regie/réalisation: Mark Robson.

Marriage on the Rocks (dt. *Dreimal nach Mexiko*, fr. *Les Inséparables*, 1965)
Dan Edwards. Director/Regie/réalisation: Jack Donohue.

Cast a Giant Shadow (dt. *Der Schatten des Giganten*, fr. *L'Ombre d'un géant*, 1966)
Vince Talmadge. Director/Regie/réalisation: Melville Shavelson.

Assault on a Queen (dt. *Überfall auf die Queen Mary*, fr. *Le Hold-up du siècle*, 1966)
Mark Brittain. Director/Regie/réalisation: Jack Donohue.

The Naked Runner (dt. *Der Mann am Draht*, fr. *Chantage au meurtre*, 1967)
Sam Laker. Director/Regie/réalisation: Sydney J. Furie.

Tony Rome (dt. *Der Schnüffler*, fr. *Tony Rome est dangereux*, 1967)
Tony Rome. Director/Regie/réalisation: Gordon Douglas.

The Detective (dt. *Der Detektiv*, fr. *Le Détective*, 1968)
Detective Joe Leland. Director/Regie/réalisation: Gordon Douglas.

Lady in Cement (dt. *Die Lady in Zement*, fr. *La Femme en ciment*, 1968)
Tony Rome. Director/Regie/réalisation: Gordon Douglas.

Dirty Dingus Magee (dt. *Der Schärfste aller Banditen*, fr. *Un beau salaud*, 1970)
Dingus Billy Magee. Director/Regie/réalisation: Burt Kennedy.

The First Deadly Sin (dt. *Die erste Todsünde*, fr. *De plein fouet*, 1980)
Edward Delaney. Director/Regie/réalisation: Brian G. Hutton.

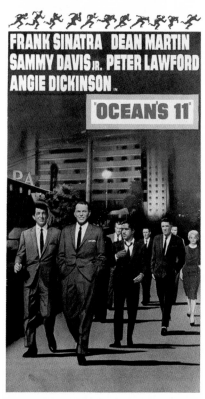

You wouldn't call it a gang. Just Danny Ocean and his 11 pals – the night they blew all the lights in Las Vegas!...

FRANK SINATRA   DEAN MARTIN
SAMMY DAVIS JR.   PETER LAWFORD
ANGIE DICKINSON in

"OCEAN'S 11"

TECHNICOLOR® PANAVISION PRESENTED BY WARNER BROS.

RICHARD CONTE · CESAR ROMERO · PATRICE WYMORE · JOEY BISHOP
AKIM TAMIROFF · HENRY SILVA guest stars RED SKELTON · GEORGE RAFT with ILKA CHASE · Screenplay by HARRY BROWN
Produced and Directed by LEWIS MILESTONE · A DORCHESTER PRODUCTION

BIBLIOGRAPHY

Adler, Bill: *Sinatra, the Man and the Myth: An Unauthorized Biography.* New American Library, 1987.

Barnes, Ken: *Sinatra and the Great Song Stylists.* Allan, 1972.

Brimhall, John: *The Essential Frank Sinatra.* Warner Books, 1998.

Burgess, Anthony: *The Man and his Music.* Avon, 1985.

Dellar, Fred: *Frank Sinatra: His Life and Times.* Omnibus. 1995.

Doctor, Gary L.: *The Sinatra Scrapbook.* Carol, 1991.

Frank, Alan G.: *Sinatra.* Hamlyn, 1978.

Freedland, Michael: *All the Way: the Biography of Frank Sinatra.* Weidenfeld & Nicholson, 1997.

Frew, Tim: *Frank Sinatra: A Life in Pictures.* MetroBooks, 1998.

Friedwald, Will: *Sinatra! The Song is You.* DaCapo, 1997.

Fuchs, Jeanne & Prigozy, Ruth (eds.): *Frank Sinatra: The Man, the Music, the Legend.* University of Rochester, 2007.

Gehman, Richard: *Sinatra and his Rat Pack.* Belmont Books, 1961.

Hamill, Pete: *Why Sinatra Matters.* Little, Brown, 1998.

Ingham, Chris: *The Rough Guide to Frank Sinatra.* Rough Guides, 2005.

Irwin, Lew: *Sinatra: A Life Remembered.* Courage Books, 1998.

Jacobs, George & Stadiem, William: *Mr. S: My Life with Frank Sinatra.* Harper, 2003

Jewell, Derek & Perry, Gerald: *Frank Sinatra.* Applause Books, 2000.

Kahn, E. J.: *The Voice: The Story of an American Phenomenon.* Musicians Press, 1947.

Kelley, Kitty: *His Way: An Unauthorized Biography Of Frank Sinatra.* Bantam, 1986.

Kuntz, Tom & Phil (eds.): *The Sinatra Files: The Secret FBI Dossier.* Three Rivers Press, 2000.

Lahr, John: *Sinatra: The Artist and the Man.* Random House, 1997.

Lake, Harriet: *On Stage with Frank Sinatra.* Creative, 1975.

Levy, Shawn: *Rat Pack Confidential.* Doubleday, 1998.

Lonstein, Albert I.: *The Compleat Sinatra.* Cameron Publications, 1970.

Mustazza, Leonard: *Ol' Blue Eyes: A Frank Sinatra Encyclopedia.* Greenwood, 1998.

Mustazza, Leonard (ed.): *Frank Sinatra and Popular Culture: Essays on an American Icon.* Praeger, 1998.

Peters, Richard: *The Frank Sinatra Scrapbook: His Life and Times in Words and Pictures.* Martin's Press, 1982.

Petkov, Steven & Mustazza, Leonard: *The Frank Sinatra Reader.* Oxford University Press, 1997.

Pignone, Charles: *Frank Sinatra: The Family Album.* Little, Brown, 2007.

Pignone, Charles: *The Sinatra Treasures.* Bulfinch, 2004.

Ridgway, John: *The Sinatrafile.* Ridgway Books, 1991.

Ringgold, Gene & McCarty, Clifford: *The Films of Frank Sinatra.* Citadel Press, 1971.

Rockwell, John: *Sinatra: An American Classic.* Random House, 1984.

Rojek, Chris: *Frank Sinatra.* Polity, 2004.

Schwarz, Ted & Sevano, Nick: *Frank Sinatra: You Only Thought You Knew Him.* Specialist Press, 2007.

Shaw, Arnold: *Sinatra: Twentieth-Century Romantic.* Holt, Rinehart and Winston, 1968.

Shaw, Arnold: *Sinatra.* Coronet Books, 1970.

Shaw, Arnold: *Sinatra, the Entertainer.* Putnam, 1982.

Sinatra, Frank: 'Me and My Music.' *Life,* 23 April 1965.

Sinatra, Frank [Foreword] in Simon, George T.: *The Big Bands.* Schirmer, 1981.

Sinatra, Nancy: *Francis Sinatra, My Father.* Doubleday, 1985.

Summers, Anthony & Swan, Robbyn: *Sinatra: The Life.* Random House, 2005.

Taraborrelli, J. Randy: *Sinatra: Behind the Legend.* Carol, 1997.

Yarwood, Guy (ed.): *Sinatra on Sinatra.* Putnam, 1983.

Zehme, Bill: *The Way You Wear Your Hat.* Harper Collins, 1997.

IMPRINT

© 2008 TASCHEN GmbH
Hohenzollernring 53, D–50672 Köln
www.taschen.com

Editor/Picture Research/Layout: Paul Duncan/Wordsmith Solutions
Editorial Coordination: Martin Holz and Mischa Gayring, Cologne
Production Coordination: Nadia Najm and Horst Neuzner, Cologne
German Translation: Thomas J. Kinne, Nauheim
French Translation: Corinne Faure-Geors, Nantes
Multilingual Production: www.arnaudbriand.com, Paris
Typeface Design: Sense/Net, Andy Disl and Birgit Reber, Cologne

Printed in Italy
ISBN 978-3-8228-2320-0

To stay informed about upcoming TASCHEN titles, please request our magazine at www.taschen.com/magazine or write to TASCHEN, Hohenzollernring 53, D-50672 Cologne, Germany, contact@taschen.com, Fax: +49-221-254919. We will be happy to send you a free copy of our magazine which is filled with information about all of our books.

All the photos in this book, except for those listed below, were supplied by The Kobal Collection.
The Jim Heiman Collection: 36/37.
Thanks to Dave Kent, Phil Moad and everybody at The Kobal Collection for their professionalism and kindness.